WEM

SOM 12/06

Field Guide to

Wild
Flowers

0129206217

How to identify flowers

> **Red flowers**
> **Pages 26–63**

This section contains flowers that are reddish in colour: from pale pink to red, and from a reddish-violet to red-brown.
(Picture: Carthusian Pink)

> **White flowers**
> **Pages 64–99**

This section contains white flowers, from snow-white to creamy, or flowers whose petals are predominantly white in colour.
(Picture: Marguerite)

> **Blue flowers**
> **Pages 100–127**

This section contains blue flowers, from pale blue to deep blue and bluish violet.

(Picture: Germander Speed-well)

For ease of identification, flowers have been divided into five colour groups.

➤ **Yellow flowers**
Pages 128–173

This section contains yellow flowers, from pale-yellow to greenish-yellow and shades of orange.
(Picture: Dandelion)

➤ **Green or inconspicuous flowers**
Pages 174–185

This section contains green flowers or plants with very small, inconspicuous flowers.
(Picture: Pineapple Weed)

FLOWER SHAPES:

Within the colour groups, flowers are also classified on the basis of the shape and symmetry of their blooms.

 Flowers with five or more petals

 Composite flowers

 Four-petalled flowers

 Flowers with mirror-symmetry

Step-by-step identification

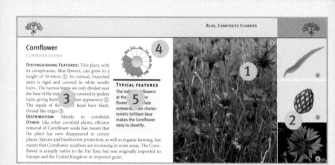

BLUE, COMPOSITE FLOWERS

Cornflower
Centaurea cyanus

DISTINGUISHING FEATURES: This plant, with its conspicuous, blue flowers, can grow to a height of 30-60cm ①. Its vertical, branched stem is rigid and covered in white woolly hairs. The narrow leaves are only divided near the base of the stem, early covered in spidery hairs, giving them a grey-green appearance ②. The sepals of the flower head have black, thread-like edges ③.

DISTRIBUTION: Mainly in cornfields

OTHER: Like other cornfield plants, efficient removal of Cornflower seeds has meant that the plant has now disappeared in certain places. Species and biodiversity protection, as well as organic farming, has meant that Cornflower numbers are increasing in some areas. The Cornflower is actually native to the Far East, but was originally imported to Europe and the United Kingdom in imported grain.

TYPICAL FEATURES
The individual flowers at the edge of the flower head radiate outwards. Their characteristic brilliant blue makes the Cornflower easy to identify.

Step 1: COMPARE WITH THE MAIN PICTURE

Each main picture is a full-size photograph of the flower species, or a photograph of its typical features, taken in its natural habitat. Easily confused species are often shown on the same page.

Step 2: IDENTIFICATION OF DISTINGUISHING FEATURES

The two illustrations and an additional photograph clearly demonstrate the distinguishing features and provide useful additional information for identification. Using these pictures will enable you to identify a species with certainty.

Step 3: IDENTIFICATION TEXT

The identification text clearly describes the important classification features of the flower. Numbered photographs and graphics provide illustrations of these features. There is also information about the distribution and habitat of the flower. This can often be a great help in identifying individual plants. Finally, the identification text also offers tips on how to distinguish a flower from other similar species.

Step 4: CALENDAR CLOCK

The grey segments indicate the main flowering period of the plant species. Due to varying climatic conditions, yearly variations in weather and different altitudes, this calendar is only a rough guide, and exceptions are possible.

■ Flowering period

Step 5: INFOBOX

The coloured Infobox provides important additional information about distinguishing or typical features. Together, these steps can help you to identify accurately the desired species.

TYPICAL FEATURES

The individual flowers at the edge of the cluster head are much larger and radiate outwards ④. The characteristic brilliant blue makes the Cornflower unmistakable.

Flowers

> A honey-bee covered in pollen from the Dandelion

The fascinating world of flowers

Flowers have long held a fascination for people with their delicate beauty, varied shapes and dazzling colours. Wild flowers, whether native or introduced, can survive in a wide range of habitats, such as fields, meadows and woodlands, but even on rubbish tips, at the roadside and on railway embankments. They also grow under what might be considered as adverse environments, such as in the snow or at very high altitudes. Flowers have developed a huge range of shapes to ensure that they can pollinate in these environments.

A wealth of species

There are 3,000 species of flowering plant in the United Kingdom. Unlike trees and shrubs, flower shoots and stems do not become woody and they brighten the countryside from

LATIN NAMES FOR CLARITY

Many species of plant have several different names, and the same name is often used for different species. For example, 'Dandelion' is a collective name for a number of similar plants. Only the Latin name can provide clarity and dispel ambiguity. In every country, no matter what language is spoken, *Taraxacum officinale* is the name of the well-known Dandelion (or Common Dandelion), and *Leontodon hispidus* is the name of the less common Rough Hawkbit.

spring to autumn. The 160 commonest species are easily found during a brief stroll through the countryside; they are comprehensively listed for you in this guide, including numerous photographs and illustrations. In addition, tips are provided on how to distinguish one flower from another when they closely resemble each other.

A logical order

In this book, flowers are listed in an order based on their obvious, external similarities. Flowers

> Foxglove

> Meadow Eyebright

> Umbels on the Wild Carrot

> Wood Forget-me-not

with very similar colouring, petal arrangement, shape or habitat are illustrated on the same page if possible. This should help you identify the flowers you are looking for and compare them with others.

The most important feature

For the average plant enthusiast, it is often hard to understand how flowering plants are classified. The most obvious feature is the flower itself, the most important part of the plant, since it ensures the proliferation and continuity of the species. The colour, shape and fragrance of blooms are designed to attract insects. They are also a great help in the identification of a plant by an untrained observer.

> A meadow ablaze with a variety of colours is a stunning sight

Flowers and their colours

The main purpose of the stunning array of flower colours is to attract pollinating insects. Patterns in different colours and designs – for example, stripes, spots or rows of dots – make flowers even more attractive to the buzzing insects. At the same time, the colour of the bloom is also the most distinguishing identification feature of a flower for humans.

Colour groups

Pure red flowers, like those of the Common Poppy, are rare in British plants. Flowers in the red section may be pale pink, or they may

> Tufted Vetch

> Wood Crane's-bill

> Meadow Crane's-bill

range in colour from carmine and crimson to pale lilac, reddish-violet and reddish-brown. Purple flowers are harder to categorise. In this book, purple flowers with a more reddish or pale-lilac colouring can be found in the red section, and bluish-purple flowers can be found in the blue section.

The white section contains snow-white or cream-coloured flowers, as well as species such as Yarrow, whose flowers can sometimes have a reddish tinge, or the Meadow Eyebright, whose flowers have a speckled pattern.

The blue section includes pale or dark blue and bluish-violet flowers. It also includes flowers with a reddish tinge, such as Tufted Vetch and Hepatica.

The yellow section includes pale-yellow to bright-yellow flowers. Yellow flowers with coloured patterns, such as the Field Pansy, can also be found in this section.

Changing colours

In some plants, the flower colour changes over time. For example, Forget-me-not and Lungwort change from pink to blue. Other species, such as Hollow-root, sometimes produce different coloured blooms on different plants. Finally, the colour of the flower may look different at different times of day and at different growing sites.

> The flowers of the Hepatica may be pale blue or reddish violet.

> Hollow-root has both reddish and white flowers

> Lungwort changes from pink to blue in colour

> The flowers of the Yarrow are often tinged with pink

11

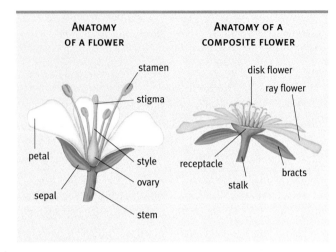

ANATOMY OF A FLOWER

stamen
stigma
petal
style
ovary
sepal
stem

ANATOMY OF A COMPOSITE FLOWER

disk flower
ray flower
receptacle
bracts
stalk

Flower shapes

Despite the wide range of possible flower shapes and forms, the basic anatomical structures can always be identified. From the outside in, they are as follows: sepals, petals, the stamen and carpel. All of these structures are specially developed for a particular purpose. When trying to distinguish between very similar species, the exact size, shape and colour of these parts are very important.

The sepals

The sepals are the outermost casing of a flower, protecting the parts of the inner flower during the bud stage. They are normally small and green. The number and shape of the sepals is an important identification feature. In some flowers, such as those of the genus *Dianthus*, the sepals grow together to form a tube-like calyx, with a characteristic rim.

The petals

The petals are the most eye-catching part of the flower and define the shape of the bloom. In many species, the petals open wide and flat, but in others they form a tube, cup or bell.

The stamen

The stamen produce great quantities of pollen grains, usually referred to simply as pollen. The number of stamen and the colour of the pollen can be very helpful when identifying flower species.

The carpel

The carpel is located in the centre

of the bloom. In most plants, the carpel forms a hollow ovary, with a long vertical extension called the style, tipped with a stigma with a sticky surface.

Strength in numbers

Many plants have small, inconspicuous flowers. In order to make themselves more notice-able, these are often not arranged individually, but instead form flower clusters that may be loose or tightly packed, making them look like one large flower.

Composite flowers

Many flowers, such as the common Daisy and Marguerite, are composite flowers and have the appearance of a single flower. On closer observation, however, it can be seen that they in fact consist of a large number of individual flowers. These are often minuscule and can only function together as a unit. The yellow flowers in the centre of the receptacle are disc flowers, and the long, white struc-tures around the outside are ray flowers (see illustration on p12).

› Field Bindweed petals are fused together

› The flowers of the Yellow Iris have mirror symmetry

› The Himalayan Balsam has symmetrical flowers

› Flowers of the Clustered Bellflower are tightly grouped together

13

Flowers and their forms

Each species of flower grows in a particular shape: some grow vertically upwards while others creep along the ground, some can grow as high as a metre while others never grow longer than a couple of centimetres. The flowers of the Ramson, for example, form on relatively long, vertical, unbranched stalks, while the flowers of the Chicory form on many-branched stems. Moss Campion has flowers with very short stems and forms a ground carpet, a characteristic that is typical of alpines. The Canadian Goldenrod, on the other hand, has eye-catching flowers, which stand upright on stems that can be as tall as a man. The Spring Crocus only grows as tall as 15cm, but the slightly branching, flowering stalks of Purple Loosestrife can stand 1.2m above their surroundings.

The stem

The stem is the part of the plant that bears the leaves. It transports water and other materials from the roots to the leaves, and then carries other nutrients from the leaves back to the roots. The stem is divided into segments by buds. It is from these buds that the leaves emerge; in some plants, these buds can also form into a side-stem. The composition of the stem is another useful identification feature. The stem can be as thin as a thread, as in the Ivy-leaved Toadflax, or as thick as a walking-stick, for example Dense-flowered Mullein and Giant Hogweed. Field Bindweed and Hedge Bindweed have flexible stems which climb upwards towards the light, using other plants and structures for support. Tufted Vetch has tendrils on its leaves which it uses for climbing.

Hollow or not?

The Dandelion stem is hollow in the centre and produces a milky, white sap. The stem of the Rough Hawkbit is filled with fluffy pith. Recognising these differences can be a great help when identifying different species.

> The Ramson has basal leaves and long, vertical flower stalks.

The shape of the stem

The shape of the stem in cross-section is also very useful for identifying a species. The stems of many plants are circular in cross-section. Some plants have more angular stems, with ridges running along their entire length. Stems can also be square in shape, either with two ribs – for example St John's Wort – or with four corners, as in the Imperforate St John's Wort.

Hairs and prickles

On many plants, the surface of the stems and leaves is not smooth, but is covered with woolly, downy, felt-like or bristly hairs. Examples are the Common Comfrey, Great Willowherb and Common Poppy. Jupiter's Distaff has slightly sticky hairs. Other plants, such as the members of the artichoke and thistle family, have many spiny and prickly growths covering all or some of their parts.

> Moss Campion forms a dense, low carpet.

> The stem of the Purple Loosestrife only branches at the top.

> The Spring Crocus is a short plant

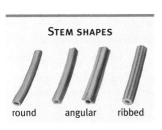

STEM SHAPES

round   angular   ribbed

> The pinnate leaves of the Silverweed have serrated edges

Flowers and their leaves

It is the task of leaves to catch as much light as possible for photosynthesis, the process of turning sunlight into energy. This energy is then used for the growth and health of the plant. Leaves are arranged so that they do not cast shade on each other, and for this reason, the upper leaves of a plant are normally smaller than the lower leaves.

Leaves for identification

Leaves can often be a help in identifying flowers, because the blooms cannot be seen all year round. The leaf shape and colour, the positioning of the leaf on the stem, and the shape of the leaf edges enable a plant to be accurately identified, even if there is no visible flower. Botanists distinguish between

several different leaf shapes, and use numerous expressions and categories to describe and classify leaf edges. A brief summary of leaf shapes and type of leaf-edge can be found in this book (see illustration opposite).

Leaf position

The leaf surface, also occasionally called the blade, is normally positioned on a stalk, but is sometimes attached directly to the stem, without a stalk. Leaves can grow from nodes, or the plant may have no nodes. If a leaf or leaf stem emerges from only one side of the node, this is called an alternating leaf arrangement. If two leaves or leaf stems emerge from a node, one on either side of the stem, this is called an opposite arrangement.

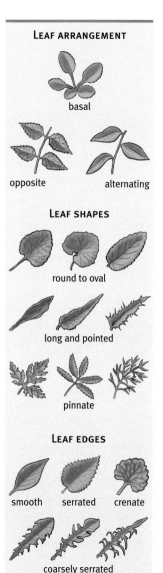

LEAF ARRANGEMENT

basal

opposite   alternating

LEAF SHAPES

round to oval

long and pointed

pinnate

LEAF EDGES

smooth   serrated   crenate

coarsely serrated

If leaves are said to be basal, this means that they grow from a node at ground level. A good example of this arrangement is the Daisy.

A variety of leaf shapes

When the leaf consists of a single part, it is called a simple leaf. If the leaf consists of several parts, it is called a composite leaf. Variations in leaf form do not just occur between species. Leaves on a single plant can often take different shapes. The basal leaves on some plants, for example on the Chicory, look very different to the leaves at the top of the stem.

For simplicity, the leaf shapes have been divided into three types – round to oval, long and pointed, and pinnate.

Leaf edges

A further important feature when identifying plants is the shape of the leaf edge. There are four main types of leaf edge – smooth edges, such as the leaves of the Lily of the Valley, serrated edges, such as the leaves of the Nettle, crenate as in Ground Ivy, and coarsely serrated, like those in the Dandelion.

17

Flowering time

Relatively few flowers are in bloom from spring to autumn. Other flowers, such as the Daisy, may be in bloom all year round, but only in places with exceptionally mild winters. In general, the flowering period of each plant is restricted to a couple of months per year.

Different flowering times

In the species descriptions in this book, details of the flowering periods of the plants make identification easier and help avoid confusion between similar species. For example, Meadow Saffron is easy to distinguish from Spring Crocus, because the former flowers in late summer and autumn, and the latter flowers in spring.

The flowering period can also be affected by external factors such as growing site, climate and weather variations, and may vary by several weeks. Later flowering periods are usually observed at higher altitudes in mountainous regions. If the weather is especially favourable, many flowers will come into bloom a second time, but these second flowers are usually significantly weaker than the first.

Whatever the weather

Even as early as February, when high ground is still under a layer of snow, the first spring flowers emerge on sunny patches of ground. Among the earliest flowers are Snowdrop, Crocus, Coltsfoot, Hepatica and Butterburr. The Primrose comes into bloom soon after.

A sudden burst of colour

Spring is the time for wild flowers. They grow rapidly and burst into flower before the trees can block their light with leaves. At this time, Lungwort, the Wood Anemone and Hollowroot cover large areas with a colourful carpet of flowers. Later, when the trees start to regrow their canopy of leaves and sunlight becomes scarce on the woodland floor, shade-loving flowers, such as Solomon's Seal and Woodruff, come into bloom.

A feast of colour

From early summer, an ever-increasing number of flowers

Coltsfoot

Cowslip

Common Violet

Scented Mayweed

Before spring

Spring

THE ANNUAL CYCLE IN THE MEADOW

In spring, the meadow is a lush, brilliant green, interspersed with the bright blooms of Daisies. In the second half of April, the red Cuckoo Flower is the first in a wave of pastel-coloured blooms, followed by the yellow Dandelion and the Meadow Buttercup. Later still, Cow Parsley, Hogweed, Marguerite and Hedge Bedstraw add their white blooms to the mix, and Ragged Robin, Red Clover and Brown Knapweed add some red shades to the mainly yellow flowers of the meadow, with Meadow Cranesbill adding some blue tones. In early summer, the

meadow is at its most colourful. After the second hay-making in late summer, the autumn meadow is once more a sea of green.

bloom in almost every habitat, except in dense woodland. The Common Poppy and the Cornflower thrive in fields of wheat and barley. Purple Loosestrife, Hedge Bedstraw, Creeping Bellflower, Lupin, Great Willowherb, Viper's Bugloss, Small Scabious and many others brighten the fields, meadows, pastures, forest clearings and roadsides with their blooms.

Autumn flowers

When autumn begins, the number of flowers decreases markedly. If the weather holds out, however, some species of flower that bloom in summer may continue to flower until the end of October or even later. Such flowers include Grove Ragwort, Tansy and Jupiter's Distaff.

Garden Lupin

Rosebay Willowherb

Grove Ragwort

Meadow Saffron

Summer

Autumn

Flower habitats

It would be pointless to look for a Wood Anemone in a meadow, and the Cornflower never grows in a wood. The Marsh Marigold cannot survive in a dry field. Some plants do not have any special requirements and can grow almost anywhere. Other plants require special habitats and will only grow in very specific conditions where they have adapted perfectly to their environment.

The basic requirements

It is normally obvious at a quick glance whether the soil in a particular habitat is dry or wet, but several other conditions are necessary for the survival of plants. A combination of the amount and type of light, availability of water, wind, soil composition and fertility of the soil, as well as a number of other factors, create a huge variety of habitats, in which different plant ecosystems establish themselves. The seriousness of the competition from neighbouring plants is also an important consideration.

Since certain species live in certain habitats, information about the distribution of the flower is very important when it comes to identification. Hence, for example, the Broad-leaved Marsh Orchid can be distinguished from the Early Purple orchid because they are found in very different habitats.

Hepatica

WOODLAND HABITAT
When in bloom, the Ramson covers the floor of lowland forests with a green-and-white carpet. Other woodland flowers include the Wood Anemone and Hepatica. As soon as the woodland canopy has its full set of leaves, the ground covering of flowers disappears once more.

Spear Thistle

MEADOW AND HEATHLAND HABITAT
Only a small amount of this habitat is original, most having been created by deforestation. Characteristic features are very little shade and a wide range of different flowers.

FIELD AND FALLOW LAND HABITATS

Fields and fallow land are also important habitats. They are quickly covered by

Common Poppy

light-loving plants, such as Gallant Soldier, Field Pennycress, Common Poppy, Chicory and many other species.

MARSHLAND HABITAT

Only certain species are adapted to survive in an excess of water.

White Water-lily

Marshes, moors, bogs and silt banks are valuable habitats in which protected species like the orchid can thrive.

Plant communities

Numerous different habitats can be identified in nature. As an example, four important types of habitat found commonly in Europe are listed on the left. As you can see, each habitat has very distinctive and very different characteristics. Each habitat is home to a specific plant community, a collection of plant species which has adapted itself to the conditions of that particular habitat. For example, meadow plants, unlike woodland plants, need a large amount of light. Fallow ground is soon covered by fast-growing plants. Subsequently, these plants die back, making room for other plants with longer lifespans. One habitat which is home to a very specialised group of plants is marshland, because only very few flowers can survive prolonged humidity.

What you can learn from colours

Rough pasture and poorly fertilised fields with nutrient-poor soil provide great growing conditions for many flowers and are therefore full of many colours. Heavily fertilised fields, on the other hand, are mainly dominated by the yellow shades of Dandelion and the Meadow Buttercup.

Flower meadows and meadow flowers

Meadows awash with a sea of flowers are one of the most beautiful sights in nature. This beauty, created by an unusually high number of different plant species, is, surprisingly, not entirely natural.

Cultivated meadows

It was humans, with their ability to change and alter the landscape, who first created the right conditions for meadows. Most meadows are cultivated land-scapes, that only maintain their appearance through regular mowing. Without hay-making, some flowers would completely disappear because other, very competitive, plants would spread aggressively. Heathland, on the other hand, is an open, grassy landscape, whose low growth is maintained by livestock grazing. The teeth of the animals play the same role as the mower.

Not all meadows are the same

Due to varying degrees of humidity, light, altitude and climatic conditions, the soil composition and other factors, several very different types of meadow have come into being, each of which is characterised by the prevalence of different species of flower.

DRY MEADOWS

Dry meadows or rough pastures normally have nutrient-poor, dry soil. They are not fertilised and are mown once a year. Spiny Restharrow (small picture), Marguerite, Meadow Clary, Nottingham Catchfly, Mouse-ear Hawkweed and Goatsbeard are all species found in dry meadows.

LOW-LIME MEADOWS

Meadows with low lime content are among the most colourful habitats, with the largest number of species, in Central Europe. Typical flowers in this habitat include the Carthusian Pink, Small Scabious, Lady's Bedstraw, Meadow Clary (small picture), Field Scabious and Harebell.

MARSHLAND

Marsh, bogs and moorland are characterised by a high water table and standing pools of water. This habitat is under threat throughout Europe, due to increasing soil drainage for cultivation and construction. Several species of orchid, Marsh Marigold (small picture), Ragged Robin and Cuckoo Flower prefer marshes.

FERTILE MEADOWS

Very high levels of fertilisation turn cultivated meadows into a habitat inhabited almost exclusively by yellow flowering plants. The normal range of meadow colours is lacking. Plant species requiring many nutrients are particularly typical of fertilised meadows, such as the Dandelion (small picture) and Buttercup.

MOUNTAIN MEADOWS

Mountain meadows are home to a large number of characteristic species, which often have particularly large flowers. They are found on and above the tree line. Typical species include Meadow Knapweed (small picture), the Globe Flower, Clustered Bellflower and Wood Crane's-bill.

MOWN FIELDS

This habitat does not contain many species of flower. Parks and gardens are well-known examples of this habitat. The very resistant and fast-growing grasses thrive here, and some flowers, for example Daisies (small picture), White Clover, Selfheal and Slender Speedwell also grow.

23

List of flowers

Cuckoo Flower
Cardamine pratensis

DISTINGUISHING FEATURES: This delicate meadow plant ① can reach a height of 30–55cm. The pinnate leaves consist of round leaflets at the base of the plant ②, but higher up the hollow stem the leaflets are long and narrow ③. The flowers are pale-pink to pinkish-red and occasionally white and are normally located at the tip of the stalk ④. They normally have four petals, but specimens with more petals are quite common. After flowering, narrow seed pods up to 4cm long form on the stalk.

TYPICAL FEATURES
When not in bloom, the Cuckoo Flower is easy to identify due to the round pinnate leaves at the base of the stalk.

DISTRIBUTION: The Cuckoo Flower is found throughout Europe in damp fertilised meadows and in light, damp deciduous woodland.

OTHER: Small amounts of foam can frequently be found on the plant, and this is known as 'cuckoo spit'. It is caused by the larvae of the Spittle Bug, which suck out the plant sap.

Coral Root
Dentaria bulbifera

DISTINGUISHING FEATURES: The plants can grow to a height of 30–50cm ①. The lower leaves are pinnate ②, but the leaves higher up on the stem are simple ③, with black, tooth-like bulbils where the leaf joins the stem ④. These onion-like buds are reproductive organs. The four pink to pale-violet petals are arranged in the shape of a cross.

TYPICAL FEATURES
The purple-black bulbils, which form where the leaf joins the stem, make the Coral Root very easy to identify.

DISTRIBUTION: This is a typical woodland wild flower. It prefers shady, deciduous woodland, mainly beechwoods, in mountainous regions at around 1,500m in altitude.

OTHER: The carpels of the pod fruits roll up suddenly when ripe, dispersing the seeds. The plant can also reproduce asexually. The bulbils in the leaf axils fall off and, when conditions are right, grow to form new plants. Sometimes these bulbils are carried away by ants, allowing the plant to spread over a larger area.

27

Rosebay Willowherb
Epilobium angustifolium

DISTINGUISHING FEATURES: This Willowherb can reach a height of 1.5m and has long, narrow leaves ② distributed over the whole stem. Vertical, candle-like flower clusters form at the tip of the stalk, which are notable for the size of the blooms and their intense pink colour ①. After flowering, numerous seeds with flight-hairs are released from long capsule fruits ③. Like the seeds of the Dandelion, these are then distributed by the wind.

DISTRIBUTION: The flower grows in forest clearings, near footpaths and on heathland. This species can reproduce very quickly and can grow densely over large areas, particularly in clearings and after fires. It was extremely common on bombed sites after World War II and is still widespread in southern England.

SIMILAR SPECIES: Alpine Willowherb *(Epilobium fleischeri)* ④, is found in the Alps, and has the same size flowers, but is only 50cm tall.

Great Willowherb
Epilobium hirsutum

DISTINGUISHING FEATURES: Great Willowherb can grow to 1.2m in height ① and has characteristic dense hairs. It has long leaves ② with an opposite arrangement. As with other species of Willowherb, the pink petals are arranged around a particularly long, thin ovary, which later develops into a seed capsule with four edges ③. The petals of the flower are always very regularly arranged.

DISTRIBUTION: Found in large numbers on riverbanks and in ditches.

OTHER: Both Rosebay Willowherb and Great Willowherb use underground shoots to cover large areas of ground. The seeds have flight-hairs and are dispersed by the wind.

SIMILAR SPECIES: *Epilobium dodonaei* ④ has very narrow leaves and is mainly found on high ground.

29

Common Poppy
Papaver rhoeas

DISTINGUISHING FEATURES: The Common Poppy is 25–90cm tall and has large, delicate flowers ①, whose bright red petals often have black flecks at the base. The large numbers of black stamens attract insects with their pollen ②. The petals normally drop within a day exposing the seed capsule, which then swells. The leaves have deep, feathery indentations ④. Leaves and stem are covered in coarse hairs.

DISTRIBUTION: Mainly in cornfields, on embankments and wasteland, where the soil has been disturbed; reductions in the use of herbicides mean that Poppy numbers are now increasing.

TYPICAL FEATURES
The fruit capsules of the Common Poppy ③ are round, egg-shaped and hairless. When ripe, the lid opens slightly, and the small, dark seeds are released into the wind.

OTHER: The leaves, stem and seed capsules produce a milky sap, which contains strong alkaloids. The bitter taste and unpleasant smell cause the flower to be avoided by grazing animals.

Speedwell
Veronica fruticulosa

DISTINGUISHING FEATURES: A herbaceous perennial which can reach a height of 10–25cm ①. The stem is woody at the base. The opposite leaves are up to 2.5cm long ② and are a narrow oval shape. Flowers are about 1cm wide, forming racemes at the end of the stem. Calyx is deeply divided into five narrow points. The uppermost of the four pale-pink, darkly-veined petals is the largest, and the lowest petal is smaller than the other two. The small, stemmed capsule fruits develop after flowering.

TYPICAL FEATURES
The flower stem and calyx of Speedwell are hairy and slightly sticky.

DISTRIBUTION: In crevices on high ground, in rocky debris, stony ground and heathland with dwarf shrubs, up to an altitude of 2,500m. The plant is often grown in rockeries as an ornamental.

SIMILAR SPECIES: Nettle-leaved Speedwell (*Veronica urticifolia*) ④ can reach a height of 70cm and has wide, serrated leaves ③. Its 8mm-wide, pale-pink flowers have dark-pink veins.

Marsh Cinquefoil
Potentilla palustris

DISTINGUISHING FEATURES: Grows to 50cm in height and has five to seven finger-like leaflets with hairs on the underside ③. The vertical stem branches at the top and has a small number of flowers ①. The purple-brown flowers are surrounded by a reddish calyx. The flower normally has five sepals and five petals, but specimens with six petals can be found.

TYPICAL FEATURES
The wide, star-shaped sepals of the Marsh Cinquefoil are much larger than the narrow petals ②.

DISTRIBUTION: As the name suggests, Marsh Cinquefoil prefers humid habitats, such as marshes, bogs and muddy banks of rivers and lakes. The plant is threatened now that so many marshes are being drained.

OTHER: The woody roots can extend up to a metre into the mud ④ and help the plant spread.

Deadly Nightshade
Atropa bella-donna

DISTINGUISHING FEATURES: Deadly Nightshade can grow to a height of 60–120cm. This eye-catching herbaceous perennial has an upright many-branched stem covered in short hairs and oval, pointed leaves with smooth edges ②. One large leaf and one smaller leaf are located on either side of the flower. The flowers form individually on short stems where the leaf joins the main stem ①. The petals are fused into a bell-shape and end in five distinct points ③; the colour varies from dark-red to brown-violet. The berry fruits are

TYPICAL FEATURES
The dark, bell-shaped flowers and the 1.5cm, shiny black berry fruits make the deadly Nightshade very easy to identify.

a shiny black colour when ripe, and they sit in a five-pointed cup ④.

DISTRIBUTION: In deforested areas and in other light areas in woods; prefers mountain woodland; on nutrient-rich soil; common.

OTHER: The fruits of the Deadly Nightshade are extremely poisonous. Just three or four berries are enough to kill a child, and 10-20 berries could kill an adult. The poisonous extract is used in medicine, however.

33

Soapwort
Saponaria officinalis

DISTINGUISHING FEATURES: Soapwort is 30–70cm tall ① and has conspicuous, carnation-like flowers, which can range in colour from almost white to pinky red. They are often arranged in dense clusters at the tip of the vertical stem, which itself is often tinged with red ④. The calyx grows to form a long, narrow tube ③. The opposite leaves are narrow and pointed and each pair of leaves is at a 90 degree angle to the last pair ②.

TYPICAL FEATURES
Soapwort's opposite leaves are divided by between three and five noticeable leaf veins ②.

DISTRIBUTION: Grows on wet, gravelly banks or in clearings.

OTHER: Soapwort is pollinated by moths, and releases a subtle aroma at dusk in order to attract insects. The plants contain a soapy substance called saponin, especially near the roots, and this used to be used for washing. Despite the unpleasant taste of the active component, Soapwort is used as a medicinal herb, externally to help cure eczema, and internally for treating respiratory, and stomach and intestinal complaints.

Purple Loosestrife
Lythrum salicaria

DISTINGUISHING FEATURES: The quadrangular stem has narrow, pointed leaves ②, which are opposite in the upper parts of the plant but are found in threes towards the base. The purple-red flowers form a dense candle-like cluster ①. In the right conditions, it can grow to over a metre in height.

TYPICAL FEATURES
Purple Loosestrife's purple flowers form on the stem in whorls, and have six, narrow lanceolate petals, with dark veins ③.

DISTRIBUTION: Purple Loosestrife grows in ditches and in damp meadows.

OTHER: The flowers produce two different types of pollen. The yellow pollen attracts insects. While the insects gather this pollen, green pollen, which the insects cannot see, sticks to their bodies and is then carried to the next plant. In folk medicine, the plant was used as a blood-clotting agent.

SIMILAR SPECIES: Marsh Woundwort (*Stachys palustris*) ④, which also grows in bogs and marshes, has long, slightly heart-shaped leaves and shorter flower clusters with lipped flowers.

Carthusian Pink
Dianthus carthusianorum

DISTINGUISHING FEATURES: The plant grows to a height of 20–60cm and has long, narrow, grass-like leaves ②. The aromatic flowers are a uniform, dark pinkish-red ① and have fine serration along the front edge. The petals are surrounded by narrow, dark sepals.

DISTRIBUTION: Carthusian Pink grows on lime-rich, dry soils. As most meadows used for agricultural purposes are heavily fertilised, this pretty plant is mainly found on steep embankments and on dry woodland edges.

TYPICAL FEATURES
The unpatterned flowers of the Carthusian Pink are normally arranged in heads of two to eight individual flowers.

OTHER: The nectar at the bottom of the calyx can only be reached by insects with a long proboscis, because the thick sepals are too thick to bite through.

SIMILAR SPECIES: *Dianthus sylvestris* on stony mountain slopes on high ground up to an altitude of 2,500m ④. It normally has only one flower per stem, and the petals are paler and have no patterning.

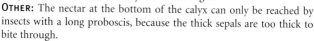

Red Campion
Silene dioica

DISTINGUISHING FEATURES: Grows to a height of 30–90cm. The thick stalk grows upright and has noticeable hairs. The broad, pointed, opposite leaves are also hairy ②. The bright pink-red flowers ① have no scent. Male and female flowers are found on different plants. Female flowers can be identified by their spherical calyx.

DISTRIBUTION: Red Campion prefers damp meadows and woods, but can also be found on woodland edges and rubbish dumps.

TYPICAL FEATURES
Red Campion flowers have five petals, but each petal has such deep indents that at a first glance, there appear to be ten petals ③.

OTHER: Bumble-bees bite through the calyx to reach the nectar. The plant is a common garden flower and it blooms abundantly.

SIMILAR SPECIES: Moss Campion *(Silene acaulis)* ④ also has pink-red flowers, and grows in mountains to form a dense carpet.

37

Ragged Robin
Lychnis flos-cuculi

DISTINGUISHING FEATURES: This tall, upright plant can reach a height of 30–60cm ①. The flowers form umbellate clusters at the tip of the stalks. Although they are very large, the petals are deeply split and look very delicate ②. After flowering, it develops egg-shaped seed capsules ③. The stalk and the narrow, opposite leaves ④ are almost hairless. The spatulate basal leaves form rosettes.

DISTRIBUTION: Ragged Robin grows in damp, nutrient-rich meadows and on flat moorland. It is often found on high ground and will cover bare soil.

TYPICAL FEATURES
The five petals are each deeply divided into four tips and are surrounded by a red-brown calyx tube with ragged indentations.

OTHER: Ragged Robin is often covered in 'cuckoo spit'. This foam is produced by the larvae of the Spittle Bug; not by cuckoos, as was once thought.

Viscid Campion
Lychnis viscaria

DISTINGUISHING FEATURES: Viscid Campion can grow to a height of 30–60cm and has purple-red flowers arranged in raceme-like clusters on the upper part of the stem ①. Each of the five petals is slightly curved, but not frayed ④. The long, hairless leaves form a basal rosette and are arranged opposite each other on the stem ②. The flat, ovoid fruit capsules ③ burst open when ripe to release the seeds.

TYPICAL FEATURES
Viscid Campion is easily recognised by the sticky ring just below the ovaries on the stem.

DISTRIBUTION: Grows on dry, acidic soil. Can be found at the edges of oak woodland, on unfertilised grassland, steep, rocky embankments and on ridges.

OTHER: The plant is so-named because of its sticky stem, which serves to repel unwanted insects, for example beetles and ants. The insects attempt to eat through the flower from below and drink the nectar. This damages the flower without in any way aiding pollination. Butterflies and bees, which fly to the flower from above, are not kept away by the sticky coating.

39

Wood Crane's-bill
Geranium sylvaticum

DISTINGUISHING FEATURES: Can reach a height of 30–70cm and has shell-like, wide open flowers, with reddish-purple petals that are white at the base ①. The fruit capsule is reminiscent of a crane's bill ② and is covered in short, silky hairs. The leaves are also conspicuous and have between five and seven lobes ③. Leaves are arranged in pairs on the stem which only branches towards the top ④.

DISTRIBUTION: Sparse, mountain forests with abundant shrubbery and on fertilised mountain meadows up to a height of 2,500m.

OTHER: The dense hairs on the stem are designed to keep insects away. The flowers only have a short life-span of about two days, and are pollinated by bees and hover-flies. The dry fruit bursts open when ripe and catapults the seeds up to a distance of 2.5m.

TYPICAL FEATURES

After flowering, the flower stems, and hence the 'crane's bill', remain upright. The Meadow Crane's-bill (p.106) is very similar, but the flower stems hang down.

Herb Robert
Geranium robertianum

DISTINGUISHING FEATURES: This variety of Crane's-bill only reaches a height of 10–20cm and has small, pinkish-red flowers ①. The petals have three whitish stripes along their length. After flowering, a bill-like fruit extends beyond the sepals. The sepals and fruits then look like the head of a stork. In autumn, the plant is noticeable because the leaf stems turn bright red, and this sometimes extends to the fine, pinnate leaves ②.

DISTRIBUTION: The species requires very little sunlight. It is therefore found even in shady woodland, in hedgerows, coppices, beside walls and in marshy ground. It can also grow in caves. Herb Robert can also, however, grow in full sunlight. It is worth noting that Herb Robert sometimes even grows on trees.

TYPICAL FEATURES

If you crush Herb Robert leaves between your fingers they release a very unpleasant smell.

SIMILAR SPECIES: Common Stork's-bill (*Erodium cicutarium*) ④ has pale-pink flowers and fine, pinnate leaves. Its seed capsules can be up to 4cm long ③ and are also shaped like a stork's bill.

41

Common Mallow
Malva sylvestris

DISTINGUISHING FEATURES: Common Mallow can grow to a height of 1m. The stem is covered in coarse hairs, and the rounded leaves have between five and seven lobes ③. Where the leaf joins the stem, pale purple flowers with dark stripes form in groups of two or more ①. These develop into small, round fruits on the end of upright stems and look rather like round cheeses ②. When ripe, the fruits fall apart in segments.

TYPICAL FEATURES
The rounded Common Mallow leaves have distinct lobes, but are not pinnate ③.

DISTRIBUTION: This conspicuous plant grows beside footpaths and fields, in hedgerows, by fences and on middens.

OTHER: Often found in cottage gardens. The leaves and flowers were used in folk remedies to treat respiratory complaints and inflammation.

SIMILAR SPECIES: Greater Musk-mallow *(Malva alcea)* ④ has rounded leaves, often with deep indentations. Its flowers always form singly where the leaf joins the stem.

Field Bindweed
Convolvulus arvensis

DISTINGUISHING FEATURES: Field Bindweed can grow to over 1m in length and has pale-pink, bell-shaped flowers with a white centre, consisting of five fused petals ④. The outside of the flower has five dark, red-violet stripes. The quick-growing stem winds itself around other plants ① or fences to keep itself upright. The capsule fruit ③ opens with two carpels.

TYPICAL FEATURES
The stemmed leaves of Field Bindweed are alternating. They are triangularly contoured and spear-shaped at the base ②.

DISTRIBUTION: This climbing plant is common in fields, near footpaths, in gardens and on fences, often in large quantities.

OTHER: The flowers are fragrant and only open during the day. They also close during bad weather. It used to be said that Field Bindweed could predict rain. The plant is regarded as a weed by gardeners and horticulturalists because it spreads uncontrollably and steals light and nutrients from cultivated plants. Weeding does little to stop the plant, because its thin roots are very long and often over a metre deep.

43

Cyclamen
Cyclamen purpurascens

DISTINGUISHING FEATURES: A herbaceous perennial growing to a height of 5–15cm. Evergreen, basal leaves grow from a spherical tuber ③ and have stems. Leaf face has a rounded shape, with a heart-shaped indentation where the stem joins the leaf. Edges are slightly serrated ②. Upper leaf surface is green and has a pale patterning; underside of the leaf is reddish. The long, leafless flower stems bear individual pinkish-red flowers. The oval, pointed petals are about 2cm long and grow upwards ①. The fruit is a spherical capsule growing on a curved, spiral stem ④.

TYPICAL FEATURES
The rounded leaves are patterned on the upper surface and the upward growing petals make the Cyclamen easy to recognise.

DISTRIBUTION: On high, rocky ground in limestone soil, up to an altitude of 2,000m; often found in large numbers. This protected plant was introduced to Europe from the Middle East during the Middle Ages.

OTHER: The tuber of the Cyclamen is very poisonous.

Meadow Saffron
Colchicum autumnale

DISTINGUISHING FEATURES: The pale reddish-lilac, star-shaped bell flowers of this poisonous plant bloom in autumn, without leaves ①. The stem and the large, long and thin leaves ② appear in spring. At the tip of the stem a capsule fruit forms with a very thin skin ③, reminiscent of a large flower bud.

TYPICAL FEATURES
Meadow Saffron's six pinkish-violet petals are fused at the base to form a flower tube about 20cm long.

DISTRIBUTION: Meadow Saffron grows in damp meadows and in light woodland.

OTHER: Beware of Meadow Saffron because it is highly poisonous. All parts of the plant contain the alkaloid colchicine, which destroys human cells. Livestock usually avoids the plant, but instances of poisoning occur when parts of the plant are found in hay.

SIMILAR SPECIES: The Spring Crocus (*Crocus albiflorus*) ④ is common in spring, and is often cultivated. It produces white to purple flowers in spring. Its flowers only have three stamen, but Meadow Saffron has six.

45

Meadow Knapweed
Centaurea jacea

DISTINGUISHING FEATURES: The stems of this plant can reach almost 1m in height and bear the reddish violet flower heads ①. The petals of the large, radiating flowers around the edge have deep indentations forming five points. The upper leaves of the plant are elongated and undivided ②; the lower leaves are sometimes divided by coarse serrations.

DISTRIBUTION: Meadow Knapweed is a common meadow plant.

OTHER: The large radiating flowers are sterile and their only purpose is to attract insects, which then pollinate the inner flowers.

> **TYPICAL FEATURES**
> The large flowers around the edge of the flower head have five points. Young plants are covered in downy hairs.

SIMILAR SPECIES: Greater Knapweed *(Centaurea scabiosa)* ④ has even larger flower heads and also has divided leaves on the stem ③. It grows on dry meadows and embankments.

Creeping Thistle
Cirsium arvense

DISTINGUISHING FEATURES: The Creeping Thistle is 20–120cm tall and can be identified by its numerous reddish-violet heads ①. These are surrounded by pointed carpels. The elongated leaves have large numbers of prickles ②. They are arranged alternately on the stem, which does not have thorns.

DISTRIBUTION: On cultivated land, beside footpaths and often found on wasteland; occasionally found in Alpine meadows.

> **TYPICAL FEATURES**
> The flower heads have a sweet musky scent which mainly attracts butterflies. They are rewarded with lots of nectar.

OTHER: The Creeping Thistle grows at an alarming rate and is disliked by farmers and gardeners. Ploughing and harrowing only helps spread the plant, because the shoots thus dispersed then grow into numerous individual plants. The fruits are an important source of food for many species of bird, however.

SIMILAR SPECIES: The Welted Thistle *(Carduus acanthoides)* ④ has flower heads which protrude from spiky carpels. It has many prickles, not only on the narrow leaves ③, but also on the stalk.

47

Spear Thistle
Cirsium vulgare

DISTINGUISHING FEATURES: The Spear Thistle can reach a height of 30–150cm. Its leaves have deep indentations and have spines ③. In addition, the stem also has spine-bearing ridges ②. The pale purple flower heads at the tip of the stem are relatively small ①.

TYPICAL FEATURES
Spiny, upward pointing carpels surround the dense flower heads of the Spear Thistle.

DISTRIBUTION: This species of thistle grows on footpaths and rubbish dumps, in light woodland and especially in soil that has been treated with lime.

OTHER: Plant-eating wild animals and grazing livestock avoid the Spear Thistle because of its spiny defences. Insects, however, visit the pollen-rich flowers in large numbers.

SIMILAR SPECIES: The Woolly Thistle (*Cirsium eriophorum*) ④ has spiny leaves with deep indentations. The flower heads are much larger and are located individually at the tip of the branching stem. The plump, basket-like carpels are covered in dense, white, woolly hairs, hence the name.

Greater Burdock
Arctium lappa

DISTINGUISHING FEATURES: This plant can reach a height of 1.8m and has a ribbed, branching stem which grows upright. The very large, stemmed leaves are rounded or slightly heart-shaped and have greyish-white hairs on their underside ②. The flower clusters also have long stems and consist of several spherical flower heads ①. The purple-red, tubular individual flowers are surrounded by hooked, crooked carpels ③.

TYPICAL FEATURES
The leaf stems and stalk of the Greater Burdock contain pith and are not hollow like other Burdock species.

DISTRIBUTION: Greater Burdock grows beside footpaths and on rubbish dumps, in clay soil that is not too dry.

OTHER: When the fruit is ripe, the carpels attach themselves to the fur of passing animals and this disperses the seeds. Greater Burdock roots contain various substances that are said to have healing powers.

SIMILAR SPECIES: Felted Burdock (*Arctium tomentosum*) ④ has a rounded calyx covered in white hairs that look like spider webs. Like all European species of Burdock, it has large, basal leaves.

49

Hemp Agrimony
Eupatorium cannabinum

DISTINGUISHING FEATURES: Hemp Agrimony can reach a height of 50–150cm and grows upright ①. It has a hairy stem. The stemmed leaves have between three and five leaflets ③ and are easily identified, even when the plant is not in flower. The pale red flower heads are located near the top of the stalk and form umbellate flower clusters ④.

TYPICAL FEATURES
The ripe fruits have a white, umbrella-like circle of hairs ② enabling them to float away on the wind.

DISTRIBUTION: The plant prefers shady, wet sites and is only found on nutrient-rich soil. It grows in dense clumps.

OTHER: The oil and the bitter substance make Hemp Agrimony a good tanning agent and an important plant in traditional medicine. The fragrance is sharp and aromatic, and flavour slightly bitter. The essential oil in the flowering plant is used for liver, spleen, gall bladder and skin complaints but it can be poisonous in large quantities. The English and Latin names derive from the fact that its leaves look like those of hemp.

Marjoram
Oregano | *Origanum vulgare*

DISTINGUISHING FEATURES: This herbaceous perennial can grow to 40cm. Its flower clusters consist of several bunches of numerous pink flowers ①. The individual flowers ② are located in the axils of small, red spathaceous bracts and have a broad top lip and a three-lobed bottom lip. The ovoid, pointed, dark-green leaves ③ have an opposite arrangement on the stem and are covered in dense, short hairs.

TYPICAL FEATURES
The large, branched flower clusters produce a powerfully aromatic fragrance.

DISTRIBUTION: The plant grows beside footpaths, on ridges and in coppices, as well as in meadows if the ground is dry.

OTHER: Marjoram contains several essential oils which can be used for treating colds, cramps and asthma. Various cultivated varieties are grown as a herb under the name of Garden Marjoram or Oregano.

SIMILAR SPECIES: Wild Basil *(Clinopodium vulgare)* ④ has flowers arranged in superimposed rings on the stem. The plant is densely hairy but has no fragrance.

51

Great Burnet
Sanguisorba officinalis

DISTINGUISHING FEATURES: Great Burnet can reach a height of 30–150cm and has unusual, dark purple, egg-shaped or oval flower heads. These are arranged in groups on the branching stem ①. The tiny individual flowers ③ do not have petals, and the four sepals are a broad, triangular shape. The alternating, pinnate leaves are a blue-green colour on the underside ②.

TYPICAL FEATURES

Great Burnet's compact, dark-red flower heads produce abundant nectar, attracting many insects ④.

DISTRIBUTION: Fens and moorland and marshy meadows where it grows in large quantities if the habitat is right.

OTHER: The botanical name of this species derives from *sanguis*, blood, and *sorbere*, to dry out. The whole plant, including the roots, is used in folk medicine as a blood-clotting agent.

Red Clover
Trifolium pratense

DISTINGUISHING FEATURES: Red Clover can grow to a height of 10–30cm. Its small, butterfly-shaped flowers ② form spherical, pinkish-red flower heads ① that smell of honey. The heads normally form in pairs at the tip of the hairy stems. Leaves usually consist of three leaflets, with a light, v-shaped stripe on the upper surface ③.

TYPICAL FEATURES

Red Clover flower heads sit just above the uppermost leaves. The flower heads on Zigzag Clover form on a short stalk above the leaves.

DISTRIBUTION: Red Clover is a very common meadow plant. It is often planted as food for grazing animals and as a winter cover crop.

OTHER: Clover leaves normally consist of three leaflets, although the legendary four-leafed clover can occasionally be found. At night, the leaves fold up. The narrow, tubular flowers are mainly pollinated by bumblebees with a long proboscis. The proboscis on a honey bee is too short to reach the nectar.

SIMILAR SPECIES: Zigzag Clover (*Trifolium medium*) ④ grows in light woodland and meadows, and is so-called because of the slightly bent stem.

53

Himalayan Balsam
Impatiens glandulifera

DISTINGUISHING FEATURES: This eye-catching plant has a fleshy stem which can grow to 2.5m in height, with a diameter of 5cm. The 4cm long flowers may be carmine red or almost white ① and they have a short spur on the lower sepal. The long stalks extend from the axils of the elongated, oval leaves ②. The leaves are arranged on the stem facing each other in pairs, or in groups of three. The leaf stalks have small pores. When ripe, the long capsules ③ burst open at the slightest touch and can disperse the seeds up to 6m distance.

TYPICAL FEATURES

The large flowers seem to sway on their thin stalks and release an intensive, sweet, quite unpleasant aroma.

DISTRIBUTION: This herbaceous perennial grows in alluvial forests and along river banks.

OTHER: The plant originates from India, but has long been grown in gardens. It also grows wild in many places, and is fully established in Europe. Its large flowers are mainly pollinated by bumblebees ④.

Spiny Restharrow
Ononis spinosa

DISTINGUISHING FEATURES: This shrub-like plant has spines and can grow to a height of 30–60cm ①. The branching stem has leaves with three leaflets as well as simple leaves in its upper reaches ③. Small, spiny shoots form where the leaves join the stem, and these bear up to three, flesh-coloured, butterfly-shaped flowers ④. The fruits are ovoid pods ②.

TYPICAL FEATURES

If you crush the leaves and flowers of Spiny Restharrow between your fingers, they release a very unpleasant aroma.

DISTRIBUTION: Grows mainly in dry habitats, such as dry meadows, embankments or pastures. Grazing animals avoid the plant, due to its sharp spines.

OTHER: The plant roots contain essential oils and tannins. An infusion made of the roots is used in folk medicine to treat rheumatism, bladder weakness and skin complaints. The plant has very deep roots, which can only be removed by harrowing. The spines also resemble the teeth of a harrow, hence the plant's name.

55

Common Selfheal

Prunella vulgaris

DISTINGUISHING FEATURES: Common Selfheal can reach a height of 10–25cm. It has red-violet flower heads at the tip of the stem ①. The individual flowers have distinct upper and lower lips ② and are surrounded by brownish sepals. The stem is quadrangular with many branches, and the leaves have an opposite, decussate arrangement ③. The plant has a tendency to form creeping shoots along the ground.

TYPICAL FEATURES

After the individual flowers have bloomed, the brown sepals remain on the plant and surround the fruit.

DISTRIBUTION: Common Selfheal is often found on wet ground, in meadows and beside footpaths.

OTHER: When the fruit is ripe, the fruit pod opens in wet weather, so that the small, triangular seeds can be washed out by rain drops.

SIMILAR SPECIES: Large Selfheal *(Prunella grandiflora)* ④ grows on dry grassland. It has larger flowers which are a more blue-violet colour.

Hedge Woundwort

Stachys sylvatica

DISTINGUISHING FEATURES: Hedge Woundwort can reach a stately height of 1.2m. The stem is branched and covered in coarse hairs. A loose head of maroon flowers forms at its tip. ①. The wide, heart-shaped leaves ③ have an opposite and decussate arrangement.

DISTRIBUTION: The plant is common in alluvial forests and other types of wet deciduous woodland from sea-level to high ground up to 1,600m.

TYPICAL FEATURES

Hedge Woundwort can be easily identified by the unpleasant aroma released when the plant is rubbed, and the maroon flowers, covered in a lighter patterning ②.

OTHER: This herbaceous perennial has long underground shoots and can cover large areas. The hairy leaves have serrated edges, reminiscent of the Nettle. They are safe to touch as they do not have any stinging hairs.

SIMILAR SPECIES: Betony *(Betonica officinalis)* ④ is smaller and grows on heathland, moors and light woodland. It has dense, red flower heads.

56

57

Heath Spotted Orchid
Dactylorhiza maculata

DISTINGUISHING FEATURES: The height of this European species of orchid can vary between 15 and 60cm. The pale reddish-mauve flowers form in dense groups at the tip of the stem ①. The stem contains pith. The side petals grow horizontally, and the flowers also have a prominent lower lip and spur. The elongated leaves are spotted with dark red ③.

TYPICAL FEATURES
The purple patterning on the lower lip of the flower is often in a distinct bow-shape ②.

DISTRIBUTION: Heath Spotted Orchid can be found in woodland and on damp meadows.
OTHER: Heath Spotted Orchid and all European species of orchid are protected. This orchid produces great numbers of seeds (several hundred thousand), but they can only germinate in combination with a species of fungus that is present in the soil. Although orchids contain no pollen, they are pollinated by insects.
SIMILAR SPECIES: Sweet-scented Orchid (*Gymnadenia conopsea*) ④ has narrower leaves without flecks and a longer spur on the flower.

Broad-leaved Marsh Orchid
Dactylorhiza majalis

DISTINGUISHING FEATURES: This European orchid can grow to a height of 10–40cm and has broad, oval leaves with dark flecks ①. The violet flowers ② at the end of the hollow stem have a lower lip with fine speckling, and a backward-facing spur. The side labella curve downwards.

TYPICAL FEATURES
Unlike the Heath Spotted Orchid, the side labella of the Broad-leaved Marsh Orchid curve downwards. The violet flower cluster also has green spathaceous bracts.

DISTRIBUTION: In damp meadows from lowland areas to high mountains.
OTHER: Broad-leaved Marsh Orchid is, like other orchid species, very rarely found in fertilised grassland. Widespread fertilisation and draining of meadows has caused orchid numbers to decrease. Orchids live in very delicate symbiosis with species of fungi, and this symbiosis cannot take place if the soil conditions are altered.
SIMILAR SPECIES: Early Purple Orchid (*Orchis mascula*) ④ prefers dry, unfertilised grassland. Its flowers ③ have dark spotting.

59

Red Foxglove
Digitalis purpurea

DISTINGUISHING FEATURES: The Red Foxglove is an eye-catching plant, partly due to the fact that it can grow to over 1m in height. The delicate purple, pale-pink, or sometimes white, flowers are bell-shaped and are speckled on the inside of the corolla tube ④. They are arranged in long, single-sided racemes ①, which open from the bottom up. The fruits develop into beak-like capsules ③. The tongue-shaped leaves ② are covered in a grey mat of hairs on the underside.

TYPICAL FEATURES
When Red Foxglove is in flower, it is unmistakable, but the leaves can be hard to identify. They are large, rough and slightly curved to form a rosette at the plant base ②.

DISTRIBUTION: Grows in woodland clearings.

OTHER: Eating the bitter-tasting leaves causes dizziness, vomiting and heart palpitations. The poisonous principle, digitalis, is still extracted to treat heart conditions.

Fumitory
Fumaria officinalis

DISTINGUISHING FEATURES: Fumitory is 10–40cm in height and only lives for a year. It has a vertical, branching stem, which is hairless and slightly ribbed. The plant has alternating, pinnate leaves on stems ②, and each leaflet is further divided into narrow segments, all ending in a point. The leaves have a blue-green sheen. The abundant pinkish-red to deep red blooms form in loose racemes at the tips of the shoots ①. They form in the axils of narrow stipules, and are

TYPICAL FEATURES
The flowers of the Fumitory have a short, thick spur, short stipules and narrow sepals.

just under 1cm long. Each flower has a spur, and the top lip also has a curved, green bump. The sepals have serrated edges. The fruit is a spherical nut.

DISTRIBUTION: This species can be commonly found on wasteland, in fields and vineyards and also in gardens. It likes nutrient-rich, loose soil.

SIMILAR SPECIES: Hollowroot *(Corydalis cava)* ④ has larger flowers with a long spur and broad, pinnate leaves ③.

61

Spotted Deadnettle
Lamium maculatum

DISTINGUISHING FEATURES: This common plant can reach a height of over 50cm ①. Its nettle-like, serrated leaves ③ form on a quadrangular stem, in an opposite and decussate arrangement ②. This nettle does not sting, hence the name. Groups of flowers with purple rolled rims can be found on the upper part of the stem. The upper lip is curved to form a hood, and the lower lip has dense flecking ④. Pure white flowers can sometime be found.

TYPICAL FEATURES
Spotted Deadnettle differs from Red Deadnettle mainly in the larger clumps of flowers it produces. It also grows taller.

DISTRIBUTION: Spotted Deadnettle grows in deciduous woodland, on woodland edges and other shady, nutrient-rich places.

OTHER: The plant remains in flower for a long time and is an important source of nectar for many different species of insect. The flowers contain tannins and essential oils which are said to have a healing effect.

Red Deadnettle
Lamium purpureum

DISTINGUISHING FEATURES: Red Deadnettle only rarely grows taller than 25cm ①. Its small flowers are pink or purplish-red. The opposite and decussate leaves are egg or heart-shaped ② with crenate edges. The angular stem and the leaves often have a red edge.

TYPICAL FEATURES
The flower of the Red Deadnettle has a wide, darkly patterned median lobe which is curved to form a lower lip ③.

DISTRIBUTION: The plant is common in heavily fertilised fields and in gardens.

OTHER: Red Deadnettle, like Spotted Deadnettle, has an unpleasant scent, but the flowers contain a sweet nectar. Unlike the Spotted Deadnettle, the flower tubes are straight and do not curve upwards. This annual plant grows very quickly. In good weather, the life cycle, from germination to seeding, may last only a few summer weeks.

SIMILAR SPECIES: Henbit Deadnettle (*Lamium amplexicaule*) ④ has leaves growing around the stem and relatively long flowers.

63

Field Penny-Cress
Thlaspi arvense

DISTINGUISHING FEATURES: Field Penny-Cress is an annual plant that can reach a height of 10–45cm ①. It is completely hairless. The arrow-shaped crenate leaves ③ form on an angular, upright and sometimes branching stem. The flowers are only 5mm in diameter ② and have four white petals which are twice as long as the sepals.

TYPICAL FEATURES

It is not the flowers of the Field Penny-Cress that are distinctive but its flat, round fruits ④, which look like coins.

DISTRIBUTION: This plant loves warmth and is often found in fields and beside footpaths, both at sea-level and in mountain regions up to an altitude of 1,300m.

OTHER: The plant was probably brought to Europe with grain from Asia. Its seeds are distributed by the wind, but also by animals and humans. The leaves have a peppery flavour and go well in salads and soups. Field Penny-Cress seeds contain a lot of oil, which can be used as salad oil.

Shepherd's Purse
Capsella bursa-pastoris

DISTINGUISHING FEATURES: Shepherd's Purse can grow to a height of 5–40cm and is an annual or biennial. The plant ① forms a basal rosette of coarsely serrated, Dandelion-like leaves ②. The undivided leaves grow sparsely on the stem ③ forming loose racemes at the tip. These then develop into heart-shaped flat seeds on stalks ④.

TYPICAL FEATURES

The most distinctive feature of Shepherd's Purse is its heart-shaped fruits ④, which stand out from the stem on thin stalks. They look slightly like leather purses, hence the name of the plant.

DISTRIBUTION: The plant is a stubborn weed, growing beside footpaths and roads, in fields, gardens and on fallow land. In mild weather, the plant can bloom and seed all year round.

OTHER: Shepherd's Purse is incredibly fertile, each plant producing up to 64,000 seeds. The leaves can be eaten as a wild vegetable or as a herb. In traditional medicine the plant is used as a blood clotting agent.

Large Bittercress
Cardamine amara

DISTINGUISHING FEATURES: This herbaceous perennial can reach a height of 30cm ①. The stem lies flat along the ground and is filled with a pith. Shoots sprout from this main stem, and these in turn form yet more shoots. The leaves are pinnate ②. The angular shoots grow upright and have racemes of small white flowers at their tips. The flowers are sometimes edged with red, a feature that is most prominent at the tip of the bud ③. The four petals are arranged facing each other in a cross and surround a mass of purple-violet stamen ④.

TYPICAL FEATURES
Large Bittercress is often confused with Watercress (p70). Its distinguishing feature is the stamens, which are purple rather than yellow.

DISTRIBUTION: Water-loving, found near brooks and springs.

OTHER: The leaves have a slightly bitter taste, giving the plant its name. The young leaves and shoots contain large amounts of vitamin C, making them a good addition to soups and salads.

Hoary Cress
Cardaria draba

DISTINGUISHING FEATURES: Hoary Cress can reach a height of 20–50cm. Its numerous small, white flowers form an umbellate cluster at the tip of the stem ①. Leaves are attached directly to the angular stem without leaf stalks and are arrow-shaped at their base ②. The inconspicuous flowers ripen into heart-shaped fruits ③.

TYPICAL FEATURES
Hoary Cress releases a sharp scent when crushed between the fingers.

DISTRIBUTION: Prefers sunny slopes, especially railway embankments, wasteland and beside footpaths. Originally from south-east Europe, but began to spread west- and northwards in the 18th century.

OTHER: Hoary Cress forms shoots from its roots, allowing it to spread very easily. Often covers large areas in a dense carpet, and can survive being mown back. Thought to be especially common along railway embankments because air currents from passing trains help spread the seeds.

SIMILAR SPECIES: Field Pepperwort (*Lepidium campestre*) ④ has more elongated racemes, and the flower clusters are not as dense.

Hedge Bedstraw
Galium album

DISTINGUISHING FEATURES: This 30–100cm tall herbaceous perennial grows very densely and is conspicuous, even from a distance ①. The very narrow leaves form in whorls of eight around the angular stem ④. The numerous, creamy-white, four-petalled flowers form dense clusters.

DISTRIBUTION: Mainly grows in grassland, beside footpaths and at the edges of coppices and woodland.

TYPICAL FEATURES

Hedge Bedstraw has a very pleasant, sweet scent. The leaves are arranged in whorls around the stem, as with all varieties of bedstraw.

OTHER: The plant attracts many bees and is valued by beekeepers because it brings a good honey harvest. Like other varieties of bedstraw, the plant contains a milk clotting agent.

SIMILAR SPECIES: Common Cleavers *(Galium aparine)* ② is an annual which prefers shady habitats. Its stems, leaves and fruit capsules are covered in barbed bristles ③.

Woodruff
Galium odoratum

DISTINGUISHING FEATURES: This perennial woodland plant can reach a height of 15–30cm. It has underground, creeping roots ② which allow it to form carpets over large areas ④. The leaves are arranged in whorls around the smooth, upright stem. The lower whorls have six leaves, the upper ones have eight ①. The stemmed flowers form in small, white umbels ③ and are bell-shaped with four points.

TYPICAL FEATURES

Woodruff has a pleasant, sweet scent which becomes more pronounced when the plant is dried.

DISTRIBUTION: In shady, deciduous woodland, particularly under beeches; widespread.

OTHER: Woodruff's characteristic scent is produced by the substance called coumarin, which can be found in all parts of the plant. This is refined and used as a flavouring for foods and drinks. Care must be taken when consuming this plant, however, as it can be poisonous in large quantities. Coumarin affects the circulation; it can cause headaches and prevent blood from clotting.

69

Garlic Mustard
Alliaria petiolata

DISTINGUISHING FEATURES: This annual plant can reach a height of up to 1m. The upright stem is usually free of branches. The basal leaves are long-stemmed and kidney-shaped ②, but leaves further up the stem are pointed, with prominent serration ①. The small, white flowers form at the end of the stem in a dense raceme ④. Each flower develops into a long, angular pod, containing many seeds ③.

TYPICAL FEATURES
Garlic Mustard is not just a random name; the plant really smells strongly of garlic.

DISTRIBUTION: Grows on nutrient-rich soils in damp coppices, woodland clearings and along footpaths in deciduous woodland. Found up to an altitude of 900m.

OTHER: All parts of this medicinal and herbal plant contain garlic and mustard oils. The finely chopped leaves have long been used to flavour dishes, due to their garlic taste. The seeds are also strongly flavoured, and can be used like mustard.

Watercress
Nasturtium officinale

DISTINGUISHING FEATURES: This 15–50cm tall evergreen plant often forms a dense ground cover ④. Its tubular, hollow stem can grow horizontally as well as vertically ①. The unpaired, pinnate leaves grow on stalks; there are between five and nine leaflets ②. The white flowers are about 1cm wide ③ and form at the ends of the stem in umbellate racemes. The four egg-shaped petals surround yellow stamens. The fruit pod is 2cm long, but only 2mm wide.

TYPICAL FEATURES
Watercress differs from Large Bittercress (p66) due to its hollow stem and yellow stamen.

DISTRIBUTION: This herbaceous perennial grows on muddy, very damp soil beside unpolluted streams and along ditches and banks. Only found in sunny locations.

OTHER: Watercress is a salad leaf that is rich in vitamin C. When blanched or cooked, the leaves lose their peppery taste and can be served as a leaf vegetable. Fresh or dried seeds can be used as a pepper-like herb. Care must be taken with eating wild watercress as it can contain liver flukes.

White Campion
Silene alba

DISTINGUISHING FEATURES: The height of this plant can vary between 30 and 100cm ①. The white, and occasionally pale pink, petals are deeply divided ③. The flowers are 2–3cm in diameter. The hairy calyx has noticeable vertical ridges. The elongated leaves form in pairs on the stem ②.

DISTRIBUTION: White Campion tends to grow on nutrient-rich, fairly dry compost heaps and beside footpaths. Common up to an altitude of 1,500m.

OTHER: White Campion forms male and female flowers on different plants.

SIMILAR SPECIES: Nottingham Catchfly (*Silene nutans*) ④ has dainty flowers, which tend to point downwards and only open in the evening. Like the White Campion, it is pollinated mainly by moths.

TYPICAL FEATURES

White Campion has sweetly-scented flowers that only open in the afternoon. The fruit capsules produced after flowering are surrounded by a convex calyx.

Bladder Campion
Silene vulgaris

DISTINGUISHING FEATURES: This herbaceous perennial can grow to a height of between 10 and 60cm, depending on its location. The elongated, pointed leaves form in pairs on the stem ②. The drooping flowers form in loose panicles at the tip of the stem ①. The white, five-petalled flowers grow in a star shape and extend beyond a very convex calyx. After flowering, this calyx persists around the seed, and has a five-pointed opening ③.

DISTRIBUTION: Common on fields, unfertilised grassland, dry meadows, beside footpaths and on embankments.

TYPICAL FEATURES

Bladder Campion's most noticeable feature is its spherical, inflated calyx ④. It is pale green with a purplish-violet, reticulate patterning.

OTHER: When squeezed, the calyx breaks with a loud pop. The flowers are open both day and night, but only produce a sweet scent in the evening. They are pollinated by moths, which suck the nectar from the flower base with their long proboscis.

Greater Stitchwort
Stellaria holostea

DISTINGUISHING FEATURES: Greater Stitchwort can reach a height of 30cm. Its narrow, evergreen leaves ③ form on the quadrangular stem. White, star-shaped flowers ① grow above the leaves, and the five petals are almost split in half. After flowering, spherical capsule fruits are produced ②.

DISTRIBUTION: This low-growing herbaceous perennial often forms a dense covering over large areas ④ of sparse woodland with lots of leafy undergrowth. It is also found in woodland edges and in hedgerows.

OTHER: New shoots grow from the leaf axils

TYPICAL FEATURES
Greater Stitchwort's white flowers form in forked clusters. The petals are longer than the sepals and surround the stamen.

of the previous year's shoots. This branching growth means that the plant can cover large areas. During harsh winters, parts of the plant above ground are killed by frost, but the roots are protected by the soil and form new shoots.

Common Stitchwort
Stellaria media

DISTINGUISHING FEATURES: Common Stitchwort is an annual plant with small, white, star-shaped flowers and a stem which grows along the ground ①. The thin stem has tiny hairs along the edge, which can be seen when held up to the light. The egg-shaped leaves ② are arranged in pairs opposite each other on the stem. After flowering, narrow seed capsules develop, which remain enclosed by the sepals ③.

DISTRIBUTION: Very common in fields, gardens, beside footpaths and in other open areas on nutrient-rich or heavily fertilised soil.

OTHER: In good conditions, the plant can

TYPICAL FEATURES
Common Stitchwort flowers have three styles and between three and eight stamens. The petals are split almost to the base and are no longer than the pointed sepals ④.

flower all year round. It is often considered to be a weed but it acts as useful ground cover in fields and gardens and keeps the soil damp, preventing loss of top soil from erosion due to wind and rain. The leaves can be eaten as a vegetable and have a mild, nutty flavour.

Wood Strawberry
Fragaria vesca

DISTINGUISHING FEATURES: Wood Strawberry grows only 8–15cm tall. It has creeping shoots above the ground and three-pointed, serrated leaves ③, with dense hairs on the underside. The white flowers ① have five round petals. The fruit develops as the receptacle swells and the sepals then stand out horizontally, or bend backwards ②.

TYPICAL FEATURES
Wood Strawberry flowers and fruits are surrounded by a green calyx. This calyx remains on the stem when the ripe fruit is picked.

DISTRIBUTION: Wood Strawberry is widespread in light, fairly dry deciduous woodland, and on woodland edges. Also grows on deforested land and beside footpaths.

OTHER: Wood Strawberries are much smaller than cultivated strawberries, but have much more flavour.

SIMILAR SPECIES: Musk Strawberry (*Fragaria moschata*) ④ can grow to 10–30cm in height, and is not only much larger than the Wood Strawberry, but has larger flowers whose stalks have perpendicular hairs.

Wood Sorrel
Oxalis acetosella

DISTINGUISHING FEATURES: Wood Sorrel is 5–15cm tall and has clover-like, three-part leaves ④ that are occasionally lightly patterned. This is caused by a plant virus. The drooping flowers form individually on long stalks ①. The five, white petals have purple veins and have a yellow spot at the base. The flower develops into a long capsule, which bursts open into five parts ③.

TYPICAL FEATURES
Wood Sorrel flowers close at night and in bad weather, and the leaves hang downwards and fold up ②.

DISTRIBUTION: Found in woods with acidic soils, especially coniferous forests.

OTHER: Wood Sorrel can grow in densely shaded areas and is often the only flowering plant on the woodland floor, the tree canopy preventing other plants from growing. The leaves taste acidic and slightly salty. They contain calcium, but also quantities of the poisonous oxalic acid. They should therefore only be eaten in small quantities.

Mouse-ear Chickweed

Cerastium holosteoides

DISTINGUISHING FEATURES: Mouse-ear Chickweed is 10–50cm tall and has small, white, star-shaped flowers ①, whose five petals are deeply split. The plant forms upright flowering shoots, and horizontal shoots which bear no flowers. The elongated leaves are covered in whitish hairs and are arranged in pairs on the stem ③.

DISTRIBUTION: In fertilised meadows, on heathland, loamy fields and beside footpaths.

OTHER: Mouse-ear Chickweed is mainly pollinated by flies. The flowers do not open in bad weather; in prolonged wet spells, the flower pollinates itself.

TYPICAL FEATURES

The small, white flowers form elongated capsule fruits ②. These spring open when they dry out. The opening has a serrated edge.

SIMILAR SPECIES: Water Chickweed (*Myosoton aquaticum*) can be found on banks and in damp habitats. Its flowers ④ form in small forked clusters. They have five styles and five divided petals; the quadrangular stem is soft and limp.

Wood Anemone

Anemone nemorosa

DISTINGUISHING FEATURES: This 15–25cm high plant has a single flower on each stem. At night and in cool weather, this flower remains closed. Three leaves with ragged edges form near the top of the stem, and the single basal leaf is also similarly serrated ③.

DISTRIBUTION: Wood Anemone often forms a carpet-like undergrowth ① in damp deciduous woodland. It also grows on unfertilised meadows.

TYPICAL FEATURES

The flowers are white on the inside and tinged with red on the outside ②. They normally have six petals.

OTHER: In early spring, when the trees are still leafless, leaves and flowers grow from the root stock. By the time the tree canopy has cut out most of the light, the Wood Anemone has already bloomed, and the parts of the plant above the ground die back. The plant is mildly poisonous.

SIMILAR SPECIES: The leaves of the Yellow Anemone (*Anemone ranunculoides*) ④ are very similar to those of the Wood Anemone. In lowland areas, both species can be found together, but they are easy to distinguish by the colour of the flowers.

79

Ramson

Allium ursinum

DISTINGUISHING FEATURES: Ramson is 10–50cm tall and smells strongly of garlic, to which it is closely related. It normally has two, elongated basal leaves, with long stalks ②. The stems are otherwise without leaves, and umbellate clusters of star-shaped, white flowers form at the tip ①. The stamen are much shorter than the petals ③.

TYPICAL FEATURES

In spring, Ramson covers woodland floors with a carpet of white flowers ④. The wood is then filled with a strong smell of garlic.

DISTRIBUTION: Ramson is typical of alluvial forests, ravine woodland and wet, deciduous woods with a mainly loamy, nutrient-rich soil.

OTHER: Young leaves can be added to salads and can be used as a flavouring in soups and with spinach. When plucking the leaves, be careful not to confuse them with those of the poisonous Lily of the Valley, or the equally poisonous Meadow Saffron. The leaves of these two plants do not smell of garlic. Ramson bulbs are also used in cooking.

Lily of the Valley

Convallaria majalis

DISTINGUISHING FEATURES: This 10–30cm tall woodland plant has two fairly broad, elongated basal leaves. The leaves and stem grow from a sheath, which later turns brown and dries out ②. The stem is leafless with an unusual flower raceme ①. The drooping, white flowers all hang on one side. The six, white petals grow together to form a bell ④. The pollinated flowers produce bright orange-red berries, slightly smaller than a pea ③.

TYPICAL FEATURES

The bell-shaped Lily of the Valley flowers release a scent that attracts many insects.

DISTRIBUTION: Lily of the Valley thrives in dry, light deciduous woodland and coppices. In very shady areas, leaves develop, but no flowers.

OTHER: Lily of the Valley is a popular garden plant but it is poisonous throughout. The roots spread through the soil, so the plant propagates quickly. In the wild, Lily of the Valley is a protected species and should not be picked or dug up.

Solomon's Seal
Polygonatum multiflorum

DISTINGUISHING FEATURES: This 30–80cm tall plant has elongated leaves, all of them growing on the same side of the stem ①. Several white, bell-shaped flowers hang in the leaf axils in a small raceme-like cluster ②. The flowers develop into blue-black berries ③.

DISTRIBUTION: In the undergrowth of shady deciduous woodland; also common in alluvial forests; mainly on nutrient-rich soil.

TYPICAL FEATURES
Solomon's Seal flowers usually hang in groups of two to five on a thin stalk in the leaf axils.

OTHER: The fruits of Solomon's Seal are poisonous. The white roots have node-like protrusions. The flowering shoots leave behind seal-like scars on the roots, hence the plant's name.

SIMILAR SPECIES: Angular Solomon's Seal (*Polygonatum odoratum*) ④, grows in sunlit locations on limestone soils. It usually has a single flower in the leaf axils.

Star of Bethlehem
Ornithogalum umbellatum

DISTINGUISHING FEATURES: Star of Bethlehem has a 10–30cm tall stem with a flower cluster of 10–20, and sometimes even more, individual flowers ①. The six milk-white petals have a green central strip on the outside ③. After flowering, club-shaped fruit capsules develop ④. Long, narrow, grass-like leaves grow from the base of the plant out of a round bulb ②.

TYPICAL FEATURES
The pretty, star-shaped flowers open wide in fine weather, but remain closed if the weather is dull.

DISTRIBUTION: Star of Bethlehem grows on dry meadows, in coppices, orchards, parks, vineyards, fields and in other grassy places. It is now widespread.

OTHER: The plant originates from the Mediterranean and therefore likes warmth. It is often cultivated for its pretty white flowers. The seeds contain oils that attract ants. The ants eat the edible stalk and disperse the seeds by carrying them away.

83

Greater Bindweed
Calystegia sepium

DISTINGUISHING FEATURES: This climbing plant can reach a height of 3m. Its thin stem winds itself around shrub twigs, and other supporting structures, including wire fences, always in an anti-clockwise direction ①. The arrow-shaped leaves ③ and the large, white, bell-shaped flowers make Greater Bindweed unmistakable. The calyx has two large bracteoles ④. Large, light-brown capsules develop after flowering ② that are largely hidden by the calyx. The fruits dry out and open in a length-wise split. The seeds are dispersed by wind or rain.

TYPICAL FEATURES
The snow-white flower cup consists of five fused petals and is surrounded by two heart-shaped leaves.

DISTRIBUTION: Greater Bindweed prefers damp habitats, such as alluvial forests, river banks, woodland edges and hedgerows; it also grows in gardens but is considered to be a noxious weed.

OTHER: The flowers are pollinated by hawk moths, which are able to reach the nectar in the base of the plant by using their long proboscis.

White Water-lily
Nymphaea alba

DISTINGUISHING FEATURES: White Water-lily is a water plant that can cover large areas ①. It has rounded, floating leaves, with a deep, prominent split. The upper surface of the leaf is a shiny green, the underside often has a reddish tint ③. The long leaf stems contain air channels and are anchored to the floor by a root as thick as the human arm. Depending on the depth of the water, the stalks may grow up to 3m long. Large, white flowers have numerous yellow stamens in the centre ④. After flowering, the plant develops berry-like fruits ②.

TYPICAL FEATURES
White Water-lily leaves have forked nerve bundles at the edges. This distinguishes the plant from the Yellow Water-lily (p142).

DISTRIBUTION: In standing water, and sometimes in slow-flowing waters. Often planted in artificial ponds and has now become wild.

OTHER: Seeds float on the water surface because a layer of air is trapped between the seed kernel and the shell. If the shell is punctured, the seed sinks to the bottom. This disperses the seeds. This plant is protected and is poisonous in all its parts.

85

Ground Elder

Aegopodium podagraria

DISTINGUISHING FEATURES: Ground Elder can reach a height of 30–100cm and produces large, flat and white flower umbels ①. Its vertical, angular forked stem is hollow and hairless. The basal leaves ② have long stems and are doubly pinnate, but the leaves further up the stem ③ have just three leaflets.

DISTRIBUTION: Ground Elder can be found in shady, damp coppices, alluvial forests, damp woodland and meadows as well as in gardens.

TYPICAL FEATURES

The leaflets on the pinnate leaves look like goat's feet. The leaves smell strongly of new-mown grass.

OTHER: The plant has deep underground shoots and carpets large areas. For this reason, it is hated and feared by gardeners as a terrible weed, because even regular weeding and soil treatment will not eradicate it.

SIMILAR SPECIES: Hairy Chervil *(Chaerophyllum hirsutum)* ④ mainly grows in mountainous regions. It has white or pink flowers and delicate, divided leaves with bristly hairs.

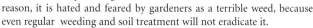

Cow Parsley

Anthriscus sylvestris

DISTINGUISHING FEATURES: This herbaceous perennial can reach a height of 60–150cm ① and has an angular stem with rough hairs near the base, while being hairless at the top. The shiny, green leaves are pinnate and divided into many tiny leaflets ③. In spring, the flower forms umbellate clusters ② with many tiny individual flowers. These flowers develop into fruits with a long, pointed end.

TYPICAL FEATURES

Cow Parsley's white individual flowers form in umbellate panicles, consisting of several smaller panicles ②.

DISTRIBUTION: Often found on heavily fertilised meadows and other nutrient-rich habitats. It often grows beneath fruit trees.

OTHER: The plant can cause an unpleasant skin irritation if touched. The roots are slightly poisonous, and can cause damage to vision if consumed.

SIMILAR SPECIES: Caraway *(Carum carvi)* ④ has relatively small, white or reddish panicles and leaves with particularly small divisions, which release the characteristic caraway smell when rubbed.

87

Wild Carrot
Daucus carota

DISTINGUISHING FEATURES: This plant can reach a height of 60–90cm and has fine, pinnate leaves ② with hair-like tips. The white, umbellate flower clusters have a single, brownish-red flower in the centre ①. The umbels are flat, dipping slightly in the middle; they are not domed. As the fruit ripens, the umbels curve upwards ③. The flowers develop into fruits with hooked spines. The aroma of Wild Carrot is like that of edible carrot.

TYPICAL FEATURES
The purplish-red to almost black single flower in the centre of the umbel ① is a distinguishing feature of the Wild Carrot.

DISTRIBUTION: In dry habitats, such as grassland, gravel pits, beside footpaths ④.

OTHER: The fine, pinnate leaves appear in the first year. The flower panicles do not form until the second year. The roots are carrot-shaped, but smaller and more woody than in the cultivated carrot which is a cross between the Wild Carrot and the Giant Carrot *(Daucus maximus)*.

Hogweed
Heracleum sphondylium

DISTINGUISHING FEATURES: Hogweed can reach a height of up to 1.5m ①. Its angular, forked stem is covered in bristles like those on a hog. It has broad umbels, consisting of individual panicles, and large lobed leaves ③. Leaf sheaths form where the leaves join the stem, and these protect the young buds.

TYPICAL FEATURES
The white flowers measure 5mm across and have a slight green or pink colouring. Only the flowers at the edge of the umbels are larger and slightly asymmetrical ②.

DISTRIBUTION: A typical plant on over-fertilised meadows. Also found in coppices, woodland clearings and deforested areas; appears after first hay-making and is one of the taller meadow plants.

OTHER: Contact with the sap of the Hogweed can cause skin irritation to people with sensitive skin.

SIMILAR SPECIES: Giant Hogweed *(Heracleum mantegazzianum)* ④ can reach a height of 5m. Substances in the plant sap can cause skin blistering when exposed to sunlight, and these blisters take a long time to heal.

89

Meadowsweet
Filipendula ulmaria

DISTINGUISHING FEATURES: Meadowsweet can reach a height of up to 2m ①. Its pinnate leaves have silvery-white hairs on the underside and consist of leaflet pairs of different sizes and a large, terminal, three-lobed leaflet ③. The flower panicle has many branches and a large number of small, yellowish-white, five-petalled flowers ②.

DISTRIBUTION: Meadowsweet mainly grows in damp meadows, in ditches and on banks.

TYPICAL FEATURES
Meadowsweet flowers release a sweet scent of almonds which persists, even when the plant is dried.

OTHER: The name Meadowsweet derives from the fact that the flower has a very sweet scent.

SIMILAR SPECIES: Wood Goatsbeard *(Aruncus dioicus)* ④ grows mainly in mountainous regions beside streams and in gorges. The yellowish-white male flowers and the pure white female flowers of this species are produced on different plants.

White Clover
Trifolium repens

DISTINGUISHING FEATURES: This fast-growing species of clover can reach 10–40cm and has small, long-stemmed, mainly white flower heads ①. The three-part leaves, hairless on the underside, grow on long stems ② and often have a light, banded patterning. The horizontal stem puts down roots at regular intervals, allowing the plant to spread quickly.

DISTRIBUTION: White Clover grows on expanses of grassland that are mown regularly, such as in parks and gardens, and often covers large areas. It needs nutrient-rich soil. The plant is remarkable for its widespread distribu-

TYPICAL FEATURES
When the White Clover flower heads have finished flowering, they hang downwards. The lower flowers turn brown.

tion. It can be found in lowland meadows, but it is just as common in the highest mountain regions, even far above the tree line.

SIMILAR SPECIES: Alsike Clover *(Trifolium hybridum)* ④ grows in marshes and in boggy areas beside footpaths. Its leaves have elongated, pointed leaflets ③. The flowers turn pale pink.

Canadian Fleabane

Conyza canadensis

DISTINGUISHING FEATURES: The stem can grow to a height of 20–90 cm and is hairless or has only very few hairs. The stem has many branches near the top. The elongated, narrow leaves ③ are covered in short, bristly hairs. The flower cluster is very tall and branching ① and normally consists of over 100 flowers, each only 3–5mm large ②. The composite flowers consist of an external row of white ray flowers, surrounding many yellow disk flowers.

DISTRIBUTION: Railways embankments, road sides, gravel banks, fields, rubbish dumps and similar wasteland; introduced into Europe from North America in the 16th century.

SIMILAR SPECIES: Daisy Fleabane *(Erigeron annuus)* ④ was also introduced from North America and has larger flower heads with longer, white or pale lilac, ray flowers.

TYPICAL FEATURES

The large flower clusters of this unpleasant-smelling plant become conspicuous in autumn when the individual composite flowers develop numerous fruits with a crown of hairs ①.

Chamomile

Camomile | Scented Mayweed

Chamomilla recutita

DISTINGUISHING FEATURES: The hairless, branching stem of Chamomile can reach a height of 15–60cm ① and has very fine, pin-nate leaves ③. The semi-spherical flower heads consist of yellow disk flowers, surrounded by white ray flowers. On older flowers, the ray flowers bend backwards ②.

DISTRIBUTION: Grows in fields, beside foot-paths, on wasteland and rubbish dumps, and also in corn fields, preferably on loamy soil with little lime.

TYPICAL FEATURES

Chamomile has a dome-shaped curving cluster of flowers ②.

OTHER: Chamomile has a strong scent and contains many substances that have made it one of the most famous medicinal plants. It is best known for its ability to reduce inflammation. Regularly drinking infusions of chamomile tea over a long period can be dangerous, however.

SIMILAR SPECIES: Scentless Chamomile *(Tripleurospermum perforatum)* ④ looks similar but the semi-spherical flower head is fuller. This species also lacks the characteristic chamomile aroma, as the name suggests.

93

Marguerite
Ox-eye Daisy | *Leucanthemum vulgare*

DISTINGUISHING FEATURES: The stem of the Marguerite is mostly hairless, has few branches if any and can reach a height of 30–70cm ①. It has elongated leaves with prominent serrations or deep lobes ②, and the stemmed, egg-shaped basal leaves ③ form a rosette. The large star-like flower attracts many insects with its nectar and forms at the end of the stem ④.

DISTRIBUTION: Marguerite is often found in meadows and on heathland, but also beside footpaths and wherever the soil is well-drained and has sufficient nutrients. The flower has a sub-species which does not grow as tall and can be found in the Alps, even above the tree line.

OTHER: Cultivated varieties of Marguerite, with large flowers, are very popular garden plants. Some of these cultivated varieties bloom very early, or twice a year.

TYPICAL FEATURES
Each of the disk flowers of the Marguerite has five equal points. The green sepals around the receptacle have dark edges.

Daisy
Bellis perennis

DISTINGUISHING FEATURES: This plant can grow to 5–15cm in height and has oval, basal leaves which form a rosette ②. A hairy, leafless stem grows out of this rosette, with a single, relatively large flower head at the tip ①. In mild weather conditions, flowers year round.

DISTRIBUTION: Very common plant; prefers areas of short grass, such as heaths, parkland, mown meadows and gardens. It can also be found beside footpaths.

TYPICAL FEATURES
The white ray flowers of the daisy often have red tinted edges. The stem is hairy. The roots are deep.

OTHER: The flower heads close up in the evening and in bad weather ③. In sunny weather, the flower heads turn to face the sun. The leaf rosette grows very close to the ground to avoid being eaten by grazing animals. Cultivated varieties with larger flowers and different colours are popular garden plants.

SIMILAR SPECIES: Daisy of the Alps (*Aster bellidiastrum*) ④ grows to a height of 30cm and is an alpine found up to an altitude of over 2,000m.

Yarrow

Achillea millefolium

DISTINGUISHING FEATURES: Yarrow can grow to 40–70cm in height ① and is noticeable due to its very dense, flat, umbellate flower clusters ④. These consist of numerous small flower heads ③ with five white, but sometimes also light-pink, ray flowers and many disc flowers in the centre. The hairy, stiff and forked stem only has branches near the top.

TYPICAL FEATURES

The lacy, double pinnate leaves ②, which are divided into numerous leaflets, are a distinguishing feature.

DISTRIBUTION: Yarrow is a common plant on meadows and heathland, beside footpaths and fields, in coppices and deforested areas, and on grassland.

OTHER: This traditional, medicinal plant is often eaten by sheep. It has a strong aromatic fragrance, caused by its essential oils and tannins. The young, soft leaves taste good in salads and leaf soups; the older, bitter leaves can be cut up small and used as seasoning.

Butterbur

Petasites hybridus

DISTINGUISHING FEATURES: This plant has white or pale-pink flowers and unusually large, round leaves, which can be up to 60cm wide and 1m tall ②. The leaves appear after the flowers and initially have a grey mat of hairs on the underside. The upright flowering shoots can be 20–50cm high. The raceme-like flower cluster ① consists of only male or female flowers, and has small stipules that are often red.

TYPICAL FEATURES

Female flowers elongate at the end of the flowering season and fruits develop in the receptacle, which has a crown of white hairs ③.

DISTRIBUTION: Butterbur typically grows on nutrient-rich banks of streams, or in alluvial forests and marshes, normally in large, dense carpets.

OTHER: Butterbur leaves are the largest of all native European flowering plants. In the Middle Ages, the creeping roots were used as a medicine against the Plague.

SIMILAR SPECIES: White Butterbur *(Petasites albus)* ④ can be found in mountain forests. It has pure white flowers and smaller leaves, with sparse, white felt-like hairs on the underside.

97

Large-flowered Eyebright
Euphrasia rostkoviana

DISTINGUISHING FEATURES: This plant rarely grows above 25cm tall ① and is conspicuous due to its two-lipped flowers with yellow and purple patterning. Some plants have pink flowers ③. The stem is hairy near the top and has many branches. The rounded leaves have serrated edges ② and are arranged opposite each other in pairs.

DISTRIBUTION: This species is mainly found on unfertilised meadows and on grassy heathland and slopes. It is common in mountainous or hilly regions and rare in lowlands.

TYPICAL FEATURES
The white flowers have a yellow spot on the three-lobed lower lip ④, and the upper lip also has some flecking.

OTHER: Large-flowered Eyebright is a semi-parasite, which uses its roots to steal nutrients from other meadow plants. Only by doing this can it obtain enough water and minerals. Infusions of the plant were used in traditional medicine to reduce eye inflammation, hence the name.

White Deadnettle
Lamium album

DISTINGUISHING FEATURES: The upright, 20–50cm tall stem of the White Deadnettle is quadrangular with deep grooves. The egg-shaped or heart-shaped, opposite leaves ② have a sharply serrated edge. The white to greenish-white flowers form whorls of between five and eight in the leaf axils ①. They have a domed upper rim forming a hood ③.

DISTRIBUTION: In nutrient-rich soil in fields and coppices, woodland edges and beside walls and fences.

TYPICAL FEATURES
Leaves have short hairs and an opposite, de-cussate arrangement. They look very similar to the Stinging Nettle (p184), but deadnettle leaves do not sting.

OTHER: As insects fly up to the plants, a lever mechanism covers them in pollen. When they fly on, they pollinate another flower.

SIMILAR SPECIES: Spotted Deadnettle (*Lamium maculatum*) ④ has purplish-red flowers, but occasionally the flowers are white. It is then hard to distinguish from the White Deadnettle. Spotted Deadnettle has a straight ring of hairs, but on the White Deadnettle these hairs grow at a slant.

99

Germander Speedwell

Veronica chamaedrys

DISTINGUISHING FEATURES: This plant can grow vertically or horizontally and reaches a height of 15–40cm. The angular stem has two rows of hairs. The rounded-to-oval leaves have an opposite arrangement and a serrated edge ③. The small, sky-blue flowers have dark-blue stripes and a yellowish or whitish centre. They form loose racemes where the upper leaves join the stem ①. The fruits are small, heart-shaped capsules.

TYPICAL FEATURES
The three petals of the Germander Speedwell flower are all the same size; the lower petal is noticeably narrower ②.

DISTRIBUTION: Widespread throughout Europe. Thrives in both lowland and mountainous regions on fertilised meadows and other nutrient-rich soils, such as heathland, beside footpaths and in coppices, hedgerows and mixed woodland.

SIMILAR SPECIES: Heath Speedwell (*Veronica officinalis*) ④ is slightly smaller and has smaller flowers arranged around a rough, hairy stem, which is sticky around the flower clusters.

Buxbaum's Speedwell

Veronica persica

DISTINGUISHING FEATURES: Buxbaum's Speedwell grows low along the ground. The triangular or rounded leaves are distinctly crenelated ②. The bright, light-blue flowers form individually on the stems ①. The lowest of the four petals is lighter in colour. In a mild climate, the flowers bloom all year round.

TYPICAL FEATURES
Buxbaum's Speedwell has sturdy, lightly haired shoots which can reach a length of 50cm. Unlike other creeping varieties of Speedwell, these shoots do not sprout roots.

DISTRIBUTION: This species of Speedwell grows well in habitats near human settlements. The plant has been found in Europe since 1805, and grows in fields, gardens and beside footpaths.

SIMILAR SPECIES: Slender Speedwell (*Veronica filiformis*) ④ is a more delicate plant with rounded leaves ③ that can sprout roots from the stem. It is a widely distributed weed and spreads quickly in pastures because the plant becomes divided and the parts root easily to form new flowers.

Spreading Bellflower
Campanula patula

DISTINGUISHING FEATURES: This species of Bellflower can reach a height of 30–60cm and has rounded, spatulate basal leaves with short stems ③. The elongated, narrow leaves grow straight from the stem ②. The petals are deeply divided into points ④ producing the characteristic bell shape of the flower, though this is less pronounced than in other Bellflower species. The flowers are arranged in loose panicles ①.

TYPICAL FEATURES
Spreading Bellflower blooms stand very upright. The flower's five points curve noticeably outwards.

DISTRIBUTION: Spreading Bellflower prefers damp, nutrient-rich habitats in lowland areas and on hillsides. It is not found in mountainous regions. Spreading Bellflower can often be found in mown meadows along with many other species; it blooms before the first hay-making.

OTHER: The flowers lower their heads in the evening and when it rains, so that the rain or dew will not wet the pollen.

Harebell
Campanula rotundifolia

DISTINGUISHING FEATURES: This 20–40cm tall plant has drooping, blue, campanulate flowers ①. The leaves on the stem ② are thin and elongated and have a smooth edge; the long-stemmed basal leaves are rounded or kidney-shaped ③. These basal leaves often wilt before the flower comes into bloom.

TYPICAL FEATURES
The rounded bells of the Harebell blooms have indentations which cut into the petal by about a third of the total length.

DISTRIBUTION: Only grows on poor soil. Found on acidic, unfertilised meadows, pastures, woodland edges, and even in rocky places. Common in Scotland, where it is known as a Bluebell (the English Bluebell is from a different plant family).

OTHER: All the Bellflowers (Campanulas) are specially adapted to insect pollination. They also have unmistakable, bell-shaped flowers, hence the name.

SIMILAR SPECIES: Peach-leaved Bellflower *(Campanula persicifolia)* ④ has wide bell flowers, on tall stems.

Creeping Bellflower
Campanula rapunculoides

DISTINGUISHING FEATURES: Creeping Bell-flower has a rough-haired stem and can grow to 30–80cm. Lower leaves are stemmed and heart-shaped, but upper leaves are narrow ② and attach directly to the stem without a leaf stalk. Five-pointed bell flowers ① are purple, but sometimes also white. After flowering, hanging capsule fruits develop on the plant ③.

TYPICAL FEATURES
Creeping Bellflower blooms are all arranged on one side of the upright stem ①.

DISTRIBUTION: On clay soil in grassland and beside footpaths, in clearings in woods and on compost heaps; prefers dry, warm locations.

OTHER: Creeping Bellflower is a very hardy plant. Its powerful roots can penetrate rocky and compacted soil. It can even grow in cracks in the asphalt of roads and in the pointing of walls.

SIMILAR SPECIES: Clustered Bellflower (*Campanula glomerata*) ④ has upward pointing flowers located in clusters at stem tips and in the upper leaf axils.

Nettle-leaved Bellflower
Campanula trachelium

DISTINGUISHING FEATURES: This sturdy Bellflower can reach a height of 1m and has noticeably large, bright blue-violet flowers at the end of its thick stem ①. The flowers form on short stems where the alternating leaves join the stem ③. The five points of the bell curve outwards and there are long hairs inside it ④. The broad, sharply serrated, nettle-like leaves ② and the stem are covered in stiff hairs.

TYPICAL FEATURES
The sharp-edged stem with its rough hairs, and the nettle-like leaves are characteristic of the Nettle-leaved Bellflower and make it easy to identify.

DISTRIBUTION: Nettle-leaved Bellflower grows in light deciduous woodland and prefers nutrient-rich soils. Found almost throughout Europe but rare in lowland areas of eastern Europe.

OTHER: The ripe fruits only release their seeds in the right weather conditions. In rainy or damp conditions, the pores of the seed capsule remain closed, but open when it is dry. The seeds can then easily be dispersed by the wind.

105

Meadow Crane's-bill
Geranium pratense

DISTINGUISHING FEATURES: Meadow Crane's-bill can reach a height of 30–60 cm and has a vertical, hairy stem. Its hand-shaped leaves have between five and seven lobes and the indentations extend almost all along the leaf base ③. The bluish-violet flowers are 3–4cm in diameter and consist of five petals, which become noticeably paler towards the centre ④. Some plants produce white flowers. The flowers form in pairs in loose clusters ①. The capsule fruits are shaped like the bill of a crane ②, hence the name.

TYPICAL FEATURES
After blooming, the flower stems of Meadow Crane's-bill curve downwards. The stem straightens once more when the plant fruits.

DISTRIBUTION: Meadow Crane's-bill needs nutrient-rich, clay and limestone soil. It grows in fertilised meadows and also beside footpaths, exclusively in hilly and mountainous areas.

OTHER: The seed capsules burst into five sections when ripe, catapulting the seeds up to 2m away from the parent plant.

Wood Forget-me-not
Myosotis sylvatica

DISTINGUISHING FEATURES: Wood Forget-me-not flowers form on a branched stem which can be 15–45cm tall ①, and which is covered in soft hairs. The narrow, oval leaves are also hairy ②. The colour of the flower can vary from sky-blue to pinkish-red to almost white. The fruit that forms after flowering is enclosed in a hairy green cup ③.

TYPICAL FEATURES
The five petals of the Wood Forget-me-not fuse at the base to form a very narrow tube. Five yellow scales form a ring at the entrance to this tube.

DISTRIBUTION: In spring, the Forget-me-not covers meadows, woodland verges and light deciduous woodland in a delicate blue carpet of colour. It only grows on nutrient-rich soil.

OTHER: The eye-catching golden-yellow colour in the centre of the flower attracts pollinating insects.

SIMILAR SPECIES: Water Forget-me-not (*Myosotis palustris*) ④ prefers damper locations and is not as hairy. The flowers form on one side of racemose clusters.

107

Lungwort
Pulmonaria officinalis

DISTINGUISHING FEATURES: Lungwort roots grow horizontally and, each spring, the new leaves and 10–20 cm tall flower stems sprout from the roots at about the same time ①. The basal leaves are an elongated egg-shape and grow on the stems; the upper leaves grow directly from the stalk ④. Leaves, stem and calyx are covered in stiff hairs. The flowers are a good 1.5cm long and change colour after flowering from pink to bluish-violet ②. After flowering, dry, slightly convex fruit capsules develop on the plant ③.

TYPICAL FEATURES
The rounded, clearly speckled leaves are characteristic of Lungwort ④.

DISTRIBUTION: Lungwort can be found in deciduous woodland, at woodland edges and in coppices up to an altitude of 1,700m.

OTHER: The colour of the flowers depends on the plant's metabolism. The flower pigment changes colour depending on the acidity of the flower cells, and this is, in turn, dependent on the age of the bloom.

Common Comfrey
Symphytum officinale

DISTINGUISHING FEATURES: Common Comfrey has bristly hairs and can grow to a height of 1.5m ①. It has purple, tubular flowers ③, which can sometimes also be whitish yellow in colour. The individual flowers have five bracts on the inside which curve inwards towards each other. The large elongated leaves ② narrow towards the ridged stalk and extend to join the next leaf.

TYPICAL FEATURES
Common Comfrey flowers can have different colours, but unlike Lungwort, all flowers on the same plant have the same colour.

DISTRIBUTION: Widespread throughout Europe and Asia, the presence of this herb is an indication of nutrient-rich soil. It grows on banks, in ditches and damp meadows and in alluvial forests.

OTHER: Common Comfrey was once believed to have the power to mend broken bones.

SIMILAR SPECIES: Tuberous Comfrey (*Symphytum tuberosum*) ④ is smaller and has yellow flowers, which bloom in April and May. It thrives in shady habitats and often forms large carpets in damp woods.

Lesser Periwinkle
Vinca minor

DISTINGUISHING FEATURES: Lesser Periwinkle has a creeping stem and can reach a height of 15–30cm ①. It has conspicuous, leathery, dark-green leaves, which are narrow and oval or egg-shaped. The leaves remain green in winter. The delicate, blue flowers form individually on upright stalks in the axils of the opposite leaves ②.

DISTRIBUTION: The Periwinkle family is very common in the tropics, but the only European member of the family is the Lesser Periwinkle. It grows in deciduous woodland, especially in hornbeam woodland and in alluvial forests containing many hard woods.

TYPICAL FEATURES
The flower of the Lesser Periwinkle fuses to form a tube ③ and the five points spread out like plates. There is a white ring at the entrance to the tube ④.

OTHER: Lesser Periwinkle is a woodland plant that needs little light. It can carpet large areas, as the creeping stems put down roots from which new plants grow. All parts of the Lesser Periwinkle are poisonous.

Hepatica
Hepatica nobilis

DISTINGUISHING FEATURES: Hepatica blooms in spring and only grows to a height of 10–20 cm ①. It has conspicuous, blue to bluish-purple flowers, which may also be pink or white. Flowers form individually on hairy stalks. Basal leaves are trilobate and liver-shaped ②, hence the name. Leaves first unfurl at the end of the flowering period, and then remain on the plant for the rest of the year, even in winter. After flowering, spherical fruits form, which are partially enclosed by three calyx-like sepals ③.

TYPICAL FEATURES
Hepatica flowers usually have between six and seven petals ④ and are surrounded by three spathaceous bracts, which look like a calyx.

DISTRIBUTION: In deciduous woodland on limestone soil, but also in pine forests, mixed woodland and in light coppices; found from sea-level to mountain regions; rare in Western Europe.

OTHER: The flowers protect themselves from the changeable spring weather by closing in the evening and in cold weather. Hepatica is considered to be slightly poisonous.

Field Scabious
Knautia arvensis

DISTINGUISHING FEATURES: The grey-green, elongated basal leaves of this 25–75cm-high plant are undivided, but the leaves on the stem have an opposite arrangement and deep indentations ②. A flat receptacle of green carpels contains several, small, bell-shaped individual flowers, each with four points, and other, larger ray flowers. The light, bluish-violet flower head forms at the end of an upright stem ①, which may be branched at the top, and which has perpendicular hairs, at least in the lower sections.

DISTRIBUTION: In dry meadows, on dry cliffs, in grassland and beside footpaths.

TYPICAL FEATURES
Field Scabious differs from Wood Scabious in that it has deeply indented leaves on the stem ②. The four-part petals on the individual flowers distinguish it from other varieties of Scabious.

SIMILAR SPECIES: Wood Scabious *(Knautia dipsacifolia)* ④ mainly grows in mountain woodland, and the points of the ray flowers are elongated. The leaves on the stem of this species are undivided ③.

Small Scabious
Scabiosa columbaria

DISTINGUISHING FEATURES: Small Scabious can grow to 20–60cm tall and has flat hairs on the stem. It has fine, pinnate leaves with crinkly hairs on the leaf stalk ②, and the basal leaves are spatulate ③. The stem is usually un-branched, and the bluish-violet flower heads form at the tip in a star-shaped receptacle ①. The 70–80 individual flowers are surrounded by a bristly calyx.

DISTRIBUTION: In unfertilised meadows and semi-dry pasture, on limestone soil.

TYPICAL FEATURES
The individual flowers of the Small Scabious have five points, interspersed with black calyx bristles.

OTHER: The fruits are enclosed in a bristly cup. When ripe, the seeds disperse using flight hairs or attach themselves to the fur of animals.

SIMILAR SPECIES: Shining Scabious *(Scabiosa lucida)* ④ is a mountain plant, whose calyx bristles are longer than those on the Small Scabious. They are interspersed between the flower petals. The leaves are normally hairless and slightly shiny.

113

Cornflower
Centaurea cyanus

DISTINGUISHING FEATURES: This plant, with its conspicuous, blue flowers can grow to a height of 30–60cm ①. The vertical, branched stem is ridged and covered in white woolly hairs. The narrow leaves are only divided near the base of the stem and are covered in spidery hairs, giving them a grey-green appearance ②. The sepals of the flower head have black, thread-like edges ③.

DISTRIBUTION: Mainly in cornfields.

OTHER: Like other cornfield plants, efficient removal of Cornflower seeds has meant that the plant has now disappeared in certain places. Species and biodiversity protection, as well as organic farming, has meant that Cornflower numbers are increasing in some areas. The Cornflower is actually native to the Far East, but was originally imported into Europe and the United Kingdom in imported grain.

TYPICAL FEATURES

The individual flowers at the edge of the flower head radiate outwards ④. Their characteristic brilliant blue makes the Cornflower easy to identify.

Chicory
Cichorium intybus

DISTINGUISHING FEATURES: This many-branched plant can reach a height of 1m ① and has a vertical, stiff, angular stem. The sky-blue flower heads are arranged in twos or threes in the axils of the upper leaves and are surrounded by green carpels. The leaves on the stem are undivided and have no stalk ②; the basal leaves have stiff hairs on their underside and are crenate or deeply lobed, reminiscent of Dandelion leaves ③.

DISTRIBUTION: In dry pastures, cultivated fields, beside footpaths and on compost heaps.

TYPICAL FEATURES

Only a few flower heads bloom on a plant at any one time. They consist of very bright, pale blue, five-pointed ray flowers ④.

OTHER: If the surrounding soil becomes very dry, Chicory sheds some of its leaves in order to reduce the surface area that would cause moisture evaporation. This protects it from drying out. Two cultivated varieties of Chicory are grown in agriculture. The roots of one variety are used as a coffee substitute. The pale leaves of the other variety is the well-known, edible Chicory which, when grown in the dark, becomes Endive.

Water Mint
Mentha aquatica

DISTINGUISHING FEATURES: Water Mint can reach a height of 30–100cm and has lilac-coloured flowers that form at the tip of the reddish, quadrangular stem ①. The egg-shaped leaves that grow in pairs on stalks facing each other have hairs on both sides ②. The leaves can sometimes also have a slightly red tint. Like most species of mint, Water Mint also has a characteristic aromatic fragrance.

TYPICAL FEATURES
Water Mint flowers grow in dense, spherical clusters at the tip of the stem and in small groups in the axils of the upper leaves ①.

DISTRIBUTION: Grows in all types of damp soils, such as marshes, damp meadows, and the banks of streams, ditches and waterways.

OTHER: Water Mint contains essential oils, from which peppermint oil is extracted. This has many uses, as a fragrance and air freshener.

SIMILAR SPECIES: Horse Mint (*Mentha longifolia*) is larger, and also grows in damp places. It has longer leaves ③ and flower clusters ④.

Lucerne
Medicago sativa

DISTINGUISHING FEATURES: This herbaceous perennial can reach a height of 30–80cm and its vertical, branching stem ① has many narrow, alternating leaves, which look like Clover leaves ②. Head-like flower racemes form at the end of the stems ④. The flowers are blue to bluish-violet and develop into spiral pods ③.

TYPICAL FEATURES
The leaflets of the three-part leaves have a slightly serrated edge. Only the terminal leaflet has a stalk ②.

DISTRIBUTION: Lucerne has been cultivated since ancient times and is mainly found in fields, as it provides good grazing for livestock. It can then spread easily to neighbouring dry meadows.

OTHER: Lucerne has very deep roots which can extend to a depth of 5m. This enables it to withstand droughts. In dry summers, the Lucerne's green leaves stand out in parched fields. The roots can produce nitrogen in the soil, so Lucerne is not merely useful as animal fodder, but also enriches the soil.

117

Blue Monkshood
Aconitum napellus

DISTINGUISHING FEATURES: Herbaceous perennial reaching 2m tall, with a vertical, straight stem ①. Stemmed leaves have five to seven deep lobes, forming a hand-shape, and these leaflets are, in turn, deeply indented ②. Dense racemes of dark-blue flowers with numerous stamens form at the tip of the stem. Two of the five petals face downwards, two extend to the side and the top leaf is shaped like a hood ③.

TYPICAL FEATURES
Unlike other species of Monkshood, the top petal of the Blue Monkshood flower is wider than it is long.

DISTRIBUTION: In mountainous woodland, among banks of vegetation in mountain regions, on heathland and upland pastures up to an altitude of 2,500m.

OTHER: Monkshood is one of Europe's most poisonous flowers. Consumption of even the smallest amount can be fatal.

SIMILAR SPECIES: Manchurian Monkshood *(Aconitum variegatum)* ④ has light-blue to violet flowers, sometimes also white or checked; the top petal is always much taller than it is wide.

Common Lupin
Lupinus polyphyllus

DISTINGUISHING FEATURES: The Common Lupin is easily identifiable due to its large, finger-shaped leaves ② and vertical, candle-like flower clusters, which can be over 50cm long ①. The bright blue to violet flowers develop into elongated pods ③.

TYPICAL FEATURES
The candle-like flower cluster of 50–80 butterfly-like individual flowers and the leaves, which are divided into 12–15 parts, make the Common Lupin easy to identify.

DISTRIBUTION: The Lupin was introduced from western North America and is often used as an ornamental flower to cover embankments and forest clearings. It often grows wild, and in some places is regarded as a successfully introduced wild flower.

OTHER: The bacteria on lupin roots binds the nitrogen in the soil and so improves it.

Garden Lupins produce flowers in a variety of colours ④ and have been bred from the Common Lupin. The seeds are poisonous unless soaked in frequent changes of water for a week. They swell into round yellow disks and are eaten as snacks in Italy and the Middle East.

118

119

Viper's Bugloss

Echium vulgare

DISTINGUISHING FEATURES: This plant grows in a two-year cycle and can be identified by its vertical flower clusters which begin as red, but turn blue ①. It can grow to a height of 1m. Its thick stem is covered in spiny, bristle-like hairs. The elongated leaves are also covered in bristles. The basal leaves grow from stalks but the leaves on the stem do not ②.

TYPICAL FEATURES

The flower buds are pink-red, but the open flowers have a blue colour ④. The flower has five pointed petals.

DISTRIBUTION: In dry locations on rubbish tips, wasteland, beside footpaths and along railway embankments.

OTHER: It the first year, Viper's Bugloss forms a rosette of narrow leaves. The flower cluster only develops in the second year. After flowering, the plant dies back as soon as the seeds are ripe, and the biennial cycle repeats itself. The flower, and in particular the fruit ③, resembles the head of a snake, hence the flower's name.

Meadow Clary

Salvia pratensis

DISTINGUISHING FEATURES: Meadow Clary can grow up to 60cm tall and forms long, vertical, candle-shaped flower clusters ①. The flowers are usually bluish-purple, but can sometimes be pale-blue, red or white, and they have a characteristic sickle-shaped, arching upper petal, and a two-lobed lower petal ②. The quadrangular stem and the elongated or round, mainly basal, leaves are hairy ③.

TYPICAL FEATURES

Meadow Clary releases an intense fragrance when the leaves are rubbed. The smell is reminiscent of Common Sage.

DISTRIBUTION: On dry meadows. Prefers steep embankments and cliffs.

OTHER: Meadow Clary is a typical plant pollinated by bees. A hanging lever mechanism helps pollination. When the insect puts its head inside the flower, it presses upon the stamen. The flower pollen then covers the back of the insect.

SIMILAR SPECIES: Common Sage (*Salvia officinalis*) ④ is a Mediterranean herb which is cultivated in gardens. It is used in cooking and is supposed to soothe sore throats.

Ground Ivy

Glechoma hederacea

DISTINGUISHING FEATURES: Ground Ivy is distinguished by its light-purple, whorl-like flower clusters. They grow in the axils of the kidney-shaped leaves ③ with their curved edges. The angular stem can be 60cm long and grows along the ground ④; the flowering shoots grow vertically ①. The petal tube is two to four times as long as the calyx and the three-lobed lower lip is dark-purple in colour ②.

DISTRIBUTION: In damp woodland, hedgerows, by fences, banks and in meadows.

OTHER: Ground Ivy used to be valued for its ability to cure fevers and wounds. The plant smells pleasantly of herbs but is mildly poisonous and is therefore very rarely used today. Bumblebees and bee sometimes gnaw through the petal tube and drink the nectar, but thi does not help the pollination process.

TYPICAL FEATURES

The creeping stem of the Ground Ivy puts down roots at intervals ④. In this respect it differs from Buxbaum's Speedwell (p100), whose horizontal stems do not sprout roots.

Bugle

Ajuga reptans

DISTINGUISHING FEATURES: Bugle can grow 7–30cm tall and has an elongated flower cluster with whorl-like blue flowers, which often grow in the axils of the small, red-brown leaves ①. Up to ten flowers can be found on each stem. Beneath the flower cluster there are two dark-green leaves, which are attached directly on to the stem ③. The basal leaves, which grow in a rosette, have a long, quadrangular stalk.

DISTRIBUTION: In fairly dry deciduous woodland and in fertilised meadows.

OTHER: Leafy shoots crawl along the ground and sprout roots from the leaf buds; this enables the plant to cover large areas quickly, protecting the soil from erosion.

TYPICAL FEATURES

Bugle's individual flowers have a wrinkled top lip, a well-formed lower lip, two side lips and a large divided central lip ②.

SIMILAR SPECIES: Blue Bugle *(Ajuga genevensis)* ④ has brilliant dark blue flower whorls and dense hairs and does not put out shoots. It grow in dry woodland and woodland edges.

123

Tufted Vetch
Vicia cracca

DISTINGUISHING FEATURES: Tufted Vetch leaves are small and pinnate, with a tendril at the tip ②, which the plant uses to climb to a height of 1.5m. The long-stemmed, racemose flower clusters ① consist of numerous bluish-purple, butterfly-shaped flowers. These develop into 2cm long, fairly plump pods ③.

DISTRIBUTION: Meadows, pastures, woodland edges, embankments and fields; common.

OTHER: The tendrils of the newly-opened leaves extend and search with a circular movement. If they come into contact with a suitable climbing medium, such as wire fences or plant stalks, they cling to it and then use it to gain a purchase for climbing.

SIMILAR SPECIES: The flowers of Wood Vetch *(Vicia sylvatica)* ④ are white to pale lilac. They form at the end of a limp, angular stalk.

TYPICAL FEATURES
Tufted Vetch can be identified by its long, bluish-purple flower racemes and angular stem, which is hairless or has sparse, flattened hairs.

Bush Vetch
Vicia sepium

DISTINGUISHING FEATURES: Bush Vetch can grow to a height of 30–60cm and has pinnate leaves, formed of four to seven pairs of elongated to egg-shaped leaflets ②. The short racemes ① only have a few butterfly-shaped individual flowers ④, which are reddish-violet in the bud, but which later change colour from purple to pale-blue. After flowering, hairless fruit pods form, which are green at first but turn shiny black when ripe ③.

DISTRIBUTION: This climbing Vetch grows in fertilised meadows and fields, as well as beside footpaths and at woodland edges.

OTHER: In wet weather, Bush Vetch releases a sweet liquid through its leaf pores, probably to help counter a pressure imbalance in the cell fluids. This additional nectar attracts ants, which then climb all over the plant. The pores are located on the underside of the stipules and look like black spots.

TYPICAL FEATURES
Each of the Bush Vetch's racemes, which form on short stalks in the leaf axils, produce up to six flowers. The sepals form a tube with points of varying lengths.

Ivy-leaved Toadflax
Cymbalaria muralis

DISTINGUISHING FEATURES: Ivy-leaved Toadflax is a low-growing or creeping plant with a branching stem. It can form a large carpet about 5–15cm high ②. The small, pale-green, rounded leaves have between five and seven lobes, and there is often a purple edge on the underside of the leaf ③. The pale violet flowers have a noticeable spur. The bright yellow spot on the lower lip attracts bees and hover flies ①.

TYPICAL FEATURES
Ivy-leaved Toadflax's long-stemmed flowers form individually in the leaf axils. The lower lip is divided in three and has two bright yellow spots at the entrance to the petal tube.

DISTRIBUTION: Originally introduced from southern Europe as an ornamental garden plant, it now grows wild in shady crevices, walls and cracks in cliffs and rocks.

OTHER: After the flowers develop into fruits, the long fruiting stalk ④ grows into dark crack or wall crevices, from which the seed is released. This ensures perfect conditions for germination.

Early Dog Violet
Wood Violet | *Viola reichenbachiana*

DISTINGUISHING FEATURES: Early Dog Violet has a violet flower ① and a spur of the same colour. Rounded oval, short-stemmed leaves ② lie on the ground but also grow on an upright stem, which can be 10–15cm in height.

TYPICAL FEATURES
Early Dog Violet flowers have five petals, which do not overlap, and a straight dark violet spur ③.

DISTRIBUTION: Early Dog Violet prefers humus-rich deciduous and mixed woodland. Found in both lowland and mountain regions.

OTHER: Delicate, striped patterning. The lowest petal enables insects to see the exact entrance to the flower from a distance, meaning that it is able to get straight to the pollen target. A large number of nectar collectors therefore only need to pause at the flower for a couple of seconds. The flowers and leaves contain essential oils that are used in alternative medicine to cure respiratory complaints.

SIMILAR SPECIES: The Common Violet (*Viola riviniana*) ④ has a pale spur on the flower and grows in light, drier woodland than the Early Dog Violet. It also grows on pastures and heathland where the soil is rich in humus.

127

Greater Celandine
Chelidonium majus

DISTINGUISHING FEATURES: The hairy stem of Greater Celandine can grow to 30–70cm in height and has many branches in its upper regions. It has divided leaves that are almost hairless and which are a striking blue-green on the underside ①. The long-stalked yellow flowers consist of four egg-shaped petals, arranged opposite each other in a cross shape and two sepals ②, which quickly fall off. Long, narrow, hairless pods form after flowering ③ and these contain many black, oily seeds.

TYPICAL FEATURES
Greater Celandine produces an orange, milky sap, which seeps from broken stems or leaves ④.

DISTRIBUTION: On compost heaps, beside footpaths and walls, and at the edges of woodland.

OTHER: The milky sap of the Greater Celandine is poisonous. It was once used for treating corns and warts. The seeds are dispersed by ants. They have a white, stalk-like protrusion, which the ants eat.

Common Tormentil
Potentilla erecta

DISTINGUISHING FEATURES: Common Tormentil is 10–30cm tall and has finger-shaped divided leaves ②. The basal leaves form a rosette, but these often wilt before the plant flowers. The upper leaves do not have a stalk and have three leaflets. They also have two smaller stipules at the base. The yellow flowers form on thin stalks in the leaf axils ①.

TYPICAL FEATURES
The flowers of Common Tormentil have black flecks on the inside and consist of four petals and four sepals.

DISTRIBUTION: Mainly in unfertilised meadows and heathland, in pastures and on woodland edges, usually on ericaceous soils.

OTHER: When the roots are cut or broken ③ they turn red at the point of damage. Substances within the plant, particularly tannins, give it medicinal properties, particularly for treating stomach complaints, and it is also used in cosmetics.

SIMILAR SPECIES: Creeping Cinquefoil (*Potentilla reptans*) ④ often grows beside footpaths, in ditches or on meadows and develops long shoots. Its large flowers have five petals.

Field Mustard
Sinapis arvensis

DISTINGUISHING FEATURES: Field Mustard is 20–60cm tall and the leaves on the stem have rough hairs and serrated edges or prominent lobes. The flower racemes are sulphurous yellow ①. Flowers develop into elongated pods, with a bill-shaped extension at the tip ②.

DISTRIBUTION: Common beside footpaths and on slopes, in fields and rubbish tips.

OTHER: The plant spread throughout Europe from the Mediterranean as land was cleared for agriculture. It is now commonly found throughout Europe, especially where the climate is mild. Field Mustard produces a large numbers of seeds and spreads rapidly. Seeds can germinate even after hundreds of years.

SIMILAR SPECIES: White Mustard *(Sinapis alba)* ④ has long-haired pods ③, but its seeds are paler in colour than those of Field Mustard. These seeds are used to make mustard commercially.

TYPICAL FEATURES
The long bill on the Field Mustard seed pod is almost round in cross-section. The seeds range in colour from reddish-brown to dark-brown.

Lady's Bedstraw
Galium verum

DISTINGUISHING FEATURES: Lady's Bedstraw is 10–70cm tall ① and is noticeable in early summer due to its whorls of narrow, needle-like leaves ② and branching panicles of golden yellow or lemon-yellow flowers ④. Individual flowers are only 3mm wide and have four pointed petals which open up like a star ③.

DISTRIBUTION: Typical of unfertilised meadows in limestone soils, beside footpaths and on coastal dunes.

TYPICAL FEATURES
The lush panicles of Lady's Bedstraw have an intense honey scent, particularly in warm weather.

OTHER: This species of Bedstraw used to be used in cheese production. The plant contains rennin, an enzyme which curdles milk and which is also found in the fourth stomach of calves. The plant is also used to obtain yellow and red dyes. Last but not least, Lady's Bedstraw also has uses in traditional medicine, for example as a diuretic. The tiny flowers produce large amounts of nectar, which provides a lot of food for bees.

131

Dark Mullein

Verbascum nigrum

DISTINGUISHING FEATURES: Dark Mullein has a two-year cycle and can grow to a height of 50–100cm ①. Leaves form on the lower half of the stem and there are many hairs on the underside, but only a few on the upper surface. They are an elongated oval shape with a heart-shaped indentation where the stalk is attached ②. The long flower clusters have yellow, wheel-shaped individual flowers, whose round petals have a purple spot at the base. Occasionally, a couple of flower clusters may form at the base. After pollination, long fruit capsules develop ③. The carpels burst open when ripe, releasing hundreds of seeds.

TYPICAL FEATURES
The anthers of Dark Mullein flowers are bright orange. Their tiny stalks are covered in purple hairs ④.

DISTRIBUTION: Dark Mullein prefers coppices, rubbish tips, deforested areas and slopes, and grows beside footpaths and on fallow grassland.

OTHER: The flowers produce very little nectar. Insects are attracted by the orange-coloured anthers.

Dense-flowered Mullein

Verbascum densiflorum

DISTINGUISHING FEATURES: Dense-flowered Mullein can grow to almost 2m and has yellow, bell-shaped flowers ③, with diameters of up to 4cm. These form in several long, racemose clusters ①. The straight, vertical stem has very few branches and a covering of woolly hairs. Leaves can be up to 40cm long and have curled edges ②. They form a rosette at the base. The leaves on the stem do not have any stalks.

TYPICAL FEATURES
Dense-flowered Mullein has leaves which attach directly to the stem. These leaves have a winged appearance and extend to join the next leaf on the stem.

DISTRIBUTION: Found in sunny deforested areas, rubbish tips, beside footpaths, in coppices and similar habitats.

OTHER: Like most other species of Mullein, Dense-flowered Mullein is a biennial. A rosette of large leaves forms in the first year, and leaves develop on the stem in the second.

SIMILAR SPECIES: Great Mullein (*Verbascum thapsus*) ④ has flowers that are only 2cm wide. It has conspicuous hairs on the stem, which has a woolly, felted appearance.

132

133

Yellow Loosestrife
Lysimachia vulgaris

DISTINGUISHING FEATURES: This plant has golden yellow flowers and a vertical stem that can reach a height of up to 1m ①. The flower racemes form at the tip of the stem and in the upper leaf axils. Each flower has five sepals with a red border and five wide petals ②. The elongated leaves normally form in whorls of three ③, but sometimes also do so in pairs or fours.

DISTRIBUTION: In damp woodland clearings and meadows, from sea-level to high mountain ranges.

TYPICAL FEATURES

The five wide-open petals look separate, but when you pluck them, it becomes clear that they are fused at the base to form a corolla.

SIMILAR SPECIES: Dotted Loosestrife *(Lysimachia punctata)* ④ has leaves on the flower clusters. The elongated leaves are arranged in whorls and have dark spots on the underside, giving the plant its name. It grows on banks and damp meadows as well as on damp woodland edges. This attractive species is often grown in cottage gardens.

St John's Wort
Hypericum perforatum

DISTINGUISHING FEATURES: Grows to a height of 30–60cm. The hairless stem has two ridges and is filled with a pith. The stem branches in the region of the flower clusters. The numerous elongated leaves have an opposite arrangement ②. The yellow flowers form together in loose clusters ①. Each flower consists of five petals and sepals and 50 or more stamen.

DISTRIBUTION: Beside footpaths, on wasteland and in forest clearings, on unfertilised meadows and marshy meadows; in lowland and mountain regions.

TYPICAL FEATURES

Against the light, the leaves appear to be perforated ②. This is caused by oil in the pores. If the petals are crushed between the fingers, a purple-red dye emerges.

OTHER: This medicinal plant is used in folk medicine to reduce inflammation and treat depression. In sunlight, substances in the plant can cause skin reactions.

SIMILAR SPECIES: Imperforate St John's Wort *(Hypericum maculatum)* ④ has a prominent hollow stem with four ridges. Its petals are covered in pore-like spots ③.

135

Cowslip
Primula veris

TYPICAL FEATURES
The Cowslip's bell-shaped flowers have an orange-coloured spot on the inside ③.

DISTINGUISHING FEATURES: An umbellate flower cluster forms at the end of the 15–30cm tall, leafless stem ①. The drooping flowers are golden-yellow and release a sweet scent. The elongated, basal leaves are crinkled ②.

DISTRIBUTION: The plant prefers dry limestone soils, such as sunny meadows and light deciduous woodland.

OTHER: The flowers of this species take two forms: one has a long style and stamen located deep in the petal tube, the other has a short style and stamen, which are situated further forward. This ensures cross-pollination between different plants.

SIMILAR SPECIES: Oxlip *(Primula elatior)* ④ grows in damper places. Its lemon-yellow flowers have no scent.

Primrose
Primula vulgaris

TYPICAL FEATURES
The Primrose has flat, open flowers and an orange-yellow spot at the entrance to the flower tube.

DISTINGUISHING FEATURES: This plant only grows to a height of 5–10cm but several flowers emerge on stalks from a basal rosette ④. The elongated, wrinkled leaves ② are grey-green and hairy on the underside. Part of the flower petals fuse to form a tube, which emerges from a narrow, five-pointed calyx ③. The upper part of the flower consists of five heart-shaped, wide-open sulphur-yellow petals that lie parallel to the ground ①. After flowering, fruits develop and the flower stalk flops to the ground.

DISTRIBUTION: Grows in deciduous woodland, at woodland edges and in hedgerows and meadows, even on nutrient-rich soil. In some regions it is severely endangered, due to modern farming methods.

OTHER: Most of our colourful garden Primulas, which are available in many different colours, originate from the Primrose. After a couple a years, garden Primulas often revert to their wild form.

137

Herb Bennet

Geum urbanum

DISTINGUISHING FEATURES: This 25–50cm tall spiky plant grows upright. The golden yellow flowers are 1.5cm in diameter and usually have five petals ①. Flowers form individually on stalks. The leaves are irregular and pinnate and the leaflets are of varying size ③. The terminal leaflet normally has three lobes.

DISTRIBUTION: In alluvial forests, coppices, beside footpaths; in nitrogen-rich soils.

OTHER: Herb Bennet roots contain a mildly toxic essential oil. The characteristic fruits ④ have a hook-like tip and attach themselves to animal fur or human clothing. This disperses the seeds.

SIMILAR SPECIES: The golden yellow flowers of Alpine Avens *(Geum montanum)* ② are much larger, being 4cm in diameter.

TYPICAL FEATURES
The fruit clusters are prickly like a hedgehog ①. They fall apart when ripe into individual fruits with a hooked tip ④.

Silverweed

Potentilla anserina

DISTINGUISHING FEATURES: Silverweed's short stems branch to form a grass-like carpet from which the leaves and flower stalks emerge. The pinnate leaves ② are green on the upper surface, and have a white felted covering of hairs on the underside. Five yellow petals extend from the calyx ①. Each flower develops into a spherical fruit cluster, consisting of several nuts ③. The plant forms rooting shoots which can be up to 50cm long.

DISTRIBUTION: On footpaths and other locations with compacted, nitrogen-rich soil.

TYPICAL FEATURES
The leaves consist of 10–20 sharply serrated leaflets, often interspersed with a tiny stipule ②.

OTHER: The flowers contain spots that reflect ultra-violet light but which are invisible to the human eye. These are used to attract insects that can see them. The small fruits are dispersed by adhering to animal fur.

SIMILAR SPECIES: Spring Cinquefoil *(Potentilla tabernaemontani)* ④ has similar flowers but the pinnate leaves are hand-shaped.

139

Acrid Buttercup
Ranunculus acris

DISTINGUISHING FEATURES: Acrid Buttercup can reach a height of 1m ①. The lower leaves have long stems and are divided to form a hand-shape. The uppermost leaves ③ are also deeply divided, but are attached directly to the stem. The flowers have five bright-yellow, circular petals, surrounding a crown of numerous stamens.

DISTRIBUTION: On heavily fertilised, damp, but not marshy, meadows and heathland.

OTHER: The plant contains a very poisonous substance with a sharp aroma, something like camphor. When dried, the poison loses its toxicity, so that Acrid Buttercup can be included in hay without harming livestock. In meadows it often grows in clumps.

SIMILAR SPECIES: Wood Buttercup (*Ranunculus nemorosus*) ④ is more hairy and prefers unfertilised meadows, deciduous and mixed woodland.

TYPICAL FEATURES
Acrid Buttercup has few if any hairs. The fruits have a short, beak-like extension and cluster in spherical heads ②.

Creeping Buttercup
Ranunculus repens

DISTINGUISHING FEATURES: This Buttercup is only 10–50cm tall and has 2–3cm large, golden-yellow flowers ①. The basal leaves grow on long stalks and are lobed. They are triangular rather than rounded ②. The numerous small fruits form at the end of the stem in a compact, spherical cluster ③.

DISTRIBUTION: Wet meadows, banks, ditches and wasteland all become covered by Creeping Buttercup, which puts out creeping shoots that form roots at the buds. In gardens, the plant can spread aggressively. It can be found in mountainous regions up to an altitude of 2,300m.

OTHER: As with all species of Buttercup, Creeping Buttercup contains toxins. Cut stems can cause skin irritations.

SIMILAR SPECIES: Bulbous Buttercup (*Ranunculus bulbosus*) ④ has sepals that bend backwards and a bulbous stem base.

TYPICAL FEATURES
The five triangular, pointed sepals of the Creeping Buttercup stand upright, very close to the broad petals.

Creeping Jenny
Lysimachia nummularia

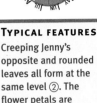

DISTINGUISHING FEATURES: Creeping Jenny has a creeping stem and forms shoots up to 50cm long, which sprout roots at the nodes. The rounded leaves form in pairs ② and are slightly reminiscent of coins. The pale yellow or bright yellow, five-petalled flowers ① grow in the middle of the stem, rather than at the tip, emerging from the leaf axils. The flowers later develop into capsule fruits.

TYPICAL FEATURES
Creeping Jenny's opposite and rounded leaves all form at the same level ②. The flower petals are about twice as long as the sepals.

DISTRIBUTION: Creeping Jenny often grows in damp places, such as damp meadows, damp footpaths or similar sites. It often covers large areas and can survive occasional drying out.

SIMILAR SPECIES: Yellow Pimpernel (*Lysimachia nemorum*) ④ has smaller and more pointed leaves. The stem grows more vertically. The flowers form individually on long thin stalks in the leaf axils ③.

Yellow Water-Lily
Brandy Bottle | *Nuphar lutea*

DISTINGUISHING FEATURES: This plant has floating leaves and creeping roots, which anchor in the silt at the bottom of the pond or stream. The leathery, egg-shaped leaves have a heart-shaped indentation where the stalk is attached ③. The plant also has soft, wrinkled underwater leaves. The flowers form individually on long stalks which extend all the way to the bottom. Five large yellow sepals surround many unobtrusive petals, containing pores than release nectar ④. The seeds of the berry-like fruits ② have a pithy flesh, which enables them to float. They are dispersed by the water.

TYPICAL FEATURES
Yellow Water-Lily's rounded leaves normally do not float. Instead, they are held just above the water level by the stalk. They release a strong smell of alcohol.

DISTRIBUTION: The Yellow Water-Lily is found on standing or slow-flowing water, where the leaves can cover large areas ①. Due to a reduction in natural water habitats, the species is endangered and highly protected.

OTHER: All parts of the plant are poisonous, especially the roots.

143

Marsh Marigold
Caltha palustris

DISTINGUISHING FEATURES: The deep-yellow, shiny flowers of the Marsh Marigold appear early in the year on a 50cm long, hollow stem that runs partially along the ground ①. The rounded leaves have a heart-shaped indentation at the base, and are dark-green and shiny ④. The upper leaves sit directly on the stem, but the basal leaves grow on a long stalk.

TYPICAL FEATURES
The shell-shaped flowers have many stamen and five golden yellow sepals, which look very much like petals.

DISTRIBUTION: In various damp habitats such as marshes and the banks of streams.

OTHER: The flowers remain open when it rains and fill with water. This pollinates them. In sunny weather, the flowers are pollinated by various insects. Marsh Marigold is slightly poisonous.

SIMILAR SPECIES: The Globe Flower (*Trollius europaeus*) ② has larger, spherical, pale yellow flowers and hand-shaped, divided leaves ③. It blooms later than the Marsh Marigold, in May and June, in damp mountain meadows.

Lesser Celandine
Ranunculus ficaria

DISTINGUISHING FEATURES: This low-growing plant only reaches a height of 5–15cm ①. Its rounded, fleshy, long-stemmed leaves are heart-shaped at the base ②. The shiny, golden-yellow, star-shaped flowers ④ form a yellow carpet in spring. During the summer, the parts of the plant above the ground die back. In Europe, Lesser Celandine does not form seeds. Instead, the plant reproduces by means of reproductive nodules, located in the leaf

TYPICAL FEATURES
Lesser Celandine flowers have 8–12 narrow petals, but normally only three sepals.

axils ③. These are blown off by heavy rain and produce new flowers.

DISTRIBUTION: Lesser Celandine often covers the ground over large areas in damp deciduous woodland, especially in alluvial forests.

OTHER: Lesser Celandine is a member of the Buttercup family and contains the same toxic substances.

145

Biting Stonecrop
Wall Pepper | *Sedum acre*

DISTINGUISHING FEATURES: Biting Stonecrop forms a clump about 5–12cm high, consisting of many stems with small, thick, fleshy leaves ②. The five-petalled flowers have pointed, fleshy petals that bend backwards ①. The fruit cluster opens like a star and contains five fruit segments ③.

DISTRIBUTION: This plant loves dry areas and quite often forms dense coverings. It is found next to walls and cliffs, in rocky places and on sandy soils.

TYPICAL FEATURES
Fresh Biting Stonecrop leaves have a sharp peppery flavour that gives the plant its name.

OTHER: The flowers produce a lot of nectar and are often visited by insects; the seeds are carried away by ants. The stem also puts down roots very readily, and this helps the plant to spread. Toxic substances in the plant irritate the mucous membranes and have a narcotic effect.

SIMILAR SPECIES: Tasteless Stonecrop *(Sedum sexangulare)* ④ has thinner leaves. It lacks Biting Stonecrop's sharp taste.

Wall Lettuce
Mycelis muralis

DISTINGUISHING FEATURES: Wall Lettuce is 60–80cm high and has irregular, pinnate leaves ②, often with a red border and a blue-green colour on the underside. Loose flower clusters form at the end of the hollow stem, containing numerous small flower heads ①. Each flower is surrounded by pale-green sepals and has a radiating crown of five light-yellow ray flowers ④. This makes it look like a simple, five-petalled flower.

TYPICAL FEATURES
If you break a stem or leaf of the Wall Lettuce, a thick, white milky sap will seep from the wound.

DISTRIBUTION: Wall Lettuce is a shade-loving plant, which prefers to grow in deciduous and pine forests with lots of leafy undergrowth. It also grows in cracks in walls, giving the plant its name. It is very common in valleys and in mountains up to an altitude of 1,700m.

OTHER: Wall Lettuce flowers are mainly pollinated by flies and bees. The small fruits have a crown of hairs ③ and are dispersed by the wind.

146

147

Canadian Goldenrod
Solidago canadensis

DISTINGUISHING FEATURES: This tall plant can grow to a height of 50–250cm ① and can often cover large areas. The hairy stem is covered in large number of narrow leaves. The tip of the stem has large numbers of small, yellow flower heads, which form branching clusters. The small fruits have a white crown of hairs ③.

TYPICAL FEATURES
The stems and underside of the leaves of Canadian Goldenrod are hairy. In the flower heads, the ray flowers and disk flowers are the same length ②.

DISTRIBUTION: Canadian Goldenrod was initially introduced to Europe from North America as an ornamental. The plant produces creeping shoots and very large numbers of seeds and can spread very quickly. It often grows wild on rubbish tips, in gardens and on riverbanks.

SIMILAR SPECIES: Early Goldenrod (*Solidago gigantea*) ④ has a stem which is free of hairs near the base. Its ray flowers are longer than the disc flowers. It is normally smaller than the Canadian Goldenrod and grows in alluvial forests, high undergrowth and beside footpaths.

Grove Ragwort
Senecio ovatus

DISTINGUISHING FEATURES: This herbaceous perennial can reach a height of 60–100cm and has oval or elongated leaves ②. The yellow flower heads are arranged in umbellate clusters at the ends of the stems ①.

TYPICAL FEATURES
Five golden-yellow, very narrow ray flowers form a star shape around 6–15 deep yellow disk flowers, which later turn brown.

DISTRIBUTION: In woods with dense undergrowth, mainly in well-lit places and in deforested areas in hills and low mountains. Found in the Alps up to an altitude of 2,000m; indicates fresh, nutrient-rich, loamy topsoil.

OTHER: The late flowering of this plant makes it is an important source of nectar for species of moth. Grove Ragwort is very poisonous. Substances in the plant can cause organ damage and may also damage genes. The plant can also make animals sick or even kill them, if eaten in large quantities.

SIMILAR SPECIES: *Senecio hercynicus* grows in the same habitats and has very narrow ray flowers ④. It has more hairs and wider leaves ③.

149

Groundsel

Senecio vulgaris

DISTINGUISHING FEATURES: This common plant can grow to different heights in different habitats, but is rarely taller than 50cm. Its flower heads form a loose cluster at the tip of the vertical stem ①. The flower heads only contain disc flowers, surrounded by a calyx of sepals ②. The flower heads develop into fruit clusters like those of the Dandelion ③. The pinnate leaves have white, matted hairs.

TYPICAL FEATURES

The sepals around the flower head are half black. The flower heads are closed most of the time and never open very wide.

DISTRIBUTION: Groundsel grows in fields, gardens and rubbish dumps. In a mild climate it can flower all year round.

OTHER: Groundsel contains toxins that can damage the liver and cause cancer.

SIMILAR SPECIES: Ragwort (*Senecio jacobea*) ④ also has yellow flower heads but these are surrounded by 13 ray flowers. Like related species, it is very poisonous.

Prickly Sow-Thistle

Sonchus asper

DISTINGUISHING FEATURES: Prickly Sow-Thistle can grow to 1m in height and has tough dark-green leaves with spiny serrated edges ①. The leaves are noticeably shiny on the upper surface. They are normally undivided and only rarely pinnate. The deep yellow flower heads form at the tip of the stem and consist of large numbers of ray flowers. These develop into silvery-white, hairy fruits ②.

TYPICAL FEATURES

If the stem of the Prickly Sow-Thistle is broken, a white, rubbery sap seeps out.

DISTRIBUTION: Prefers loamy, nutrient-rich fields, but also grows in gardens and rubbish dumps.

OTHER: The small fruits have a crown of long hairs that acts like a parachute and allows them to be carried on the wind. Ants also contribute to seed dispersal. The plant produces a milky sap, and despite its coarse leaves it is a valuable fodder for livestock.

SIMILAR SPECIES: Common Sow-Thistle(*Sonchus oleraceus*) ④ has no tough spines. Unlike the Prickly Sow-Thistle, it has distinct pinnate leaves ③; the upper leaves are attached directly to the stem.

Rough Hawksbeard

Crepis biennis

DISTINGUISHING FEATURES: Rough Hawksbeard can reach a height of 50–120cm and has conspicuous, branching flower heads similar to those of the Dandelion ①. The elongated, serrated leaves ② are attached to the branched stem. After flowering, numerous fruits develop in the flower receptacle, each with a crown of white, flexible hairs, which act as a parachute and aid wind dispersal.

TYPICAL FEATURES

The stem and leaves of Rough Hawksbeard produce a white, milky sap. The serrated edges on the leaves tend to point down.

DISTRIBUTION: Common in fertilised meadows and beside footpaths.

OTHER: In its first year, Rough Hawksbeard only develops a cluster of leaves. These leaves survive the winter and produce a flower cluster in the second year. Fruits and seeds can develop without pollination.

SIMILAR SPECIES: Smooth Hawksbeard *(Crepis capillaris)* ④ has smaller reddish flower heads. The leaves are narrower and their serrated edges point upwards ③.

Nipplewort

Lapsana communis

DISTINGUISHING FEATURES: This upright plant can reach a height of 30–100cm and develops a loose flower cluster consisting of several small, pale-yellow flower heads ①. The individual flowers are all ray flowers ③, with two rows of sepals. The main stem has a few hairs, produces a milky sap and has many branches, particularly near the top. The side stems grow upwards at a steep angle ④. The lower leaves have clear indentations ② and the upper leaves are elongated. Fruits have no crown of hairs.

TYPICAL FEATURES

Nipplewort can be identified by its characteristic leaf shape, with two smaller side lobes below the large end lobes ②.

DISTRIBUTION: Nipplewort grows in alluvial forests, clearings, on nutrient-rich fields, beside footpaths and on rubbish tips. In thrives in heavily fertilised grassland and is an indication that the soil contains a lot of nitrogen. It is a common weed in gardens.

OTHER: If the sky is cloudy, the flowers remain shut. Even on sunny days, the flowers only open in the mornings.

153

Corn Sow-Thistle
Sonchus arvensis

DISTINGUISHING FEATURES: This spiny plant can reach a height of 50–150cm and has elongated, pinnate leaves ②. Its vertical stem only branches below the flower clusters. The golden-yellow flower head is reminiscent of the Dandelion ④ and consists solely of ray flowers ①. The numerous fruits all have a crown of hairs, and are dispersed by the wind. Together they form a spherical, white-haired fruit cluster ③. The plant has creeping roots and can cover large areas of ground.

TYPICAL FEATURES
Corn Sow-Thistle leaves surround half of the stem. The flower heads and stalks have small, yellow and sticky pores.

DISTRIBUTION: Corn Sow-Thistle grows on loamy fields, beside footpaths, on banks and in ditches. It is not found above 1,500m.

OTHER: The plant has a milky sap and is used as fodder for geese. Corn Sow-Thistle is poisonous to humans.

Common Hawkbit
Leontodon hispidus

DISTINGUISHING FEATURES: The yellow flower heads of the 15–50cm tall Common Hawkbit grow from a rosette of leaves ②. They sit individually on a thin, leafless stalk that is covered in coarse hairs ①. Unlike the common Dandelion (p156) the stem is not hollow.

DISTRIBUTION: Common Hawkbit is a meadow plant. It is found in fertilised meadows, boggy meadows and semi-dry grassland. This undemanding plant can be found from sea-level to high mountain ranges.

TYPICAL FEATURES
The flower heads of Common Hawkbit droop before flowering ③. They consist of a large number of yellow ray flowers. The outer ray flowers sometimes have a red stripe on the outside.

OTHER: The flowers remain open from early morning to early afternoon. The seeds are dispersed with the help of a parachute-like crown of hairs on the fruit.

SIMILAR SPECIES: *Leontodon helveticus* ④ is an alpine that grows on mountain heathland. Extremely rare outside the Alps. The orange-yellow flower heads stand upright, even before flowering.

154

155

Dandelion
Taraxacum officinale

DISTINGUISHING FEATURES: Dandelion is 10–50cm tall and has a leaf rosette of irregular, deeply divided leaves ④. The stem is hollow and leafless and there is a single, large flower head, with up to 200 ray flowers ①. The flower only opens in sunshine, and is closed in the evening and in bad weather. After flowering, it forms a spherical fruit cluster ② the seeds being born on small, downy 'umbrellas' ③. These fruits break away when ripe, and are carried away by the wind.

TYPICAL FEATURES
If you pluck off the flower head, a milky sap will ooze from the hollow stem. This sap is slightly sticky and tastes bitter.

DISTRIBUTION: Grows in large numbers on nutrient-rich soils, such as meadows (especially fertilised meadows), heathland, beside footpaths and in gardens.

OTHER: In spring, the young leaves are eaten in salads. The leaves are valued in folk medicine as a diuretic and are said to cleanse the blood.

Goatsbeard
Tragopogon pratensis

DISTINGUISHING FEATURES: Can grow to 30–60cm in height and has a wide flower head with pale yellow ray flowers ①, surrounded by narrow, green sepals ④. The tips of the anthers are dark-violet. The thin stem is covered in many grass-like, narrow leaves ②. After flowering, a large seed-head forms that is reminiscent of the fruit cluster of the Dandelion ③.

TYPICAL FEATURES
Goatsbeard's flower heads only open in sunny weather and close by midday.

DISTRIBUTION: Goatsbeard loves the warmth and prefers meadows of loose clay or loamy soil, without any standing water. It also grows in semi-dry grassland and beside footpaths. Found in the Alps up to an altitude of 1,700m.

OTHER: Goatsbeard is so-named because when the fruit cluster is closed, the protruding white hairs look like the beard of a goat. The young shoots used to be prepared like asparagus and eaten as a vegetable. The same is true for the root, which tastes something like salsify.

157

Coltsfoot
Tussilago farfara

DISTINGUISHING FEATURES: Coltsfoot has a 15cm high stem, and each stem is topped by a single flower head ①. A row of narrow ray flowers surrounds the central disc of flowers. The stem has scaly leaves ③. The large, basal leaves with matted hairs on the underside only emerge after flowering. They have long stalks and a heart-shaped, almost pentagonal contour ②. The crown of hairs on the fruits, which looks like an umbrella, is very long ④.

TYPICAL FEATURES

When flowering, Coltsfoot is leafless. Its stem is covered in leaf scales.

DISTRIBUTION: Coltsfoot grows wherever there is no established undergrowth, particularly on rubbish tips, along waysides or beside fields.

OTHER: Coltsfoot's ability to cure coughs has been known since antiquity. An overdose of this medicinal plant can cause liver damage, however.

Mouse-ear Hawkweed
Hieracium pilosella

DISTINGUISHING FEATURES: This plant can grow from 5cm to 30cm in height and often forms large carpets. Its pale yellow or sulphurous yellow flower heads consist solely of ray flowers ① and form on a leafless stalk above a rosette of basal leaves ②. The flowers are surrounded on the outside by short sepals ④. The blue-green leaves are elongated or oval in shape. They have long hairs on the upper surface and on the edges, and the underside is covered in silvery-white, felt-like hairs ③.

TYPICAL FEATURES

Mouse-ear Hawkweed has ray flowers which often have a red stripe on the underside.

DISTRIBUTION: Mouse-ear Hawkweed is typically to be found on sunny, warm, unfertilised and dry grassland, on heathland and beside footpaths

OTHER: In dry weather, the leaves roll up. The white underside of the leaf then reflects the sunlight and prevents the plant from over-heating. The plant is thus protected from drying out. The flower heads open from the morning to the early afternoon, but only in sunny weather.

159

Tansy
Tanacetum vulgare

DISTINGUISHING FEATURES: Tansy can reach 1.50m in height and has a woody stem, which branches in the upper parts. The yellow, button-like flowers ② form umbellate flower clusters ①. The leaves are alternating and pinnate and consist of twelve pairs of heavily serrated leaves of different sizes ③.

DISTRIBUTION: Common on rubbish tips and railway embankments, also beside footpaths, riverbanks and at coppice edges.

TYPICAL FEATURES

Tansy's fine, pinnate leaves are reminiscent of fern leaves. When crushed, they release a very aromatic fragrance.

OTHER: Tansy is a traditional medicinal plant. It is poisonous in large quantities, however, and used to be used as a vermifuge. It is used in agriculture today to keep away pests and to strengthen cultivated plants.

SIMILAR SPECIES: *Tanacetum corymbosum* ④ has similar leaves and white flowers. Unlike Tansy, the leaves have no scent.

Black Medick | Nonsuch
Medicago lupulina

DISTINGUISHING FEATURES: Black Medick has up to 50 tiny yellow flowers forming a spherical flower head ①. This plant is partly low-growing, but also forms a stem which can be 50cm long. The stem has clover-like leaves, with very few hairs. The individual leaflets are slightly serrated.

DISTRIBUTION: On meadows and rubbish tips. It generally prefers low ground, beside footpaths and waysides but can also be found in hilly regions.

TYPICAL FEATURES

When the petals fall off after blooming, the black, wrinkled fruits become visible, clustering together to form a fruit head ③.

OTHER: Unlike species of Clover (*Trifolium* species), the petals of Black Medick are not shed after flowering. The plant is sometimes also grown as animal fodder or as a fertilising plant.

SIMILAR SPECIES: Hop Trefoil (*Trifolium campestre*) ④ has larger flower heads, whose petals do not fall off after flowering ②. It does not have crinkled fruit pods.

Meadow Pea
Lathyrus pratensis

DISTINGUISHING FEATURES: Meadow Pea is 30–60cm high and has yellow, racemose clusters ①. They consist of individual butterfly-like flowers ③. The angular stem has short, flat hairs and pinnate leaves with tendrils ②, but the plant is a poor climber. The narrow leaves have prominent veins on the underside. The fruit pods blacken when ripe ④.

DISTRIBUTION: This species of pea grows on nutrient-rich fertilised meadows, marshy meadows and moorland.

TYPICAL FEATURES
Up to 12 butterfly-like flowers form on the Meadow Pea at the end of a flower stalk which rises prominently above the narrow pinnate leaves.

OTHER: Unlike the garden pea, the fruits of this plant are flat. The roots have nodes, as is common in many pod-bearing plants. These are caused by bacteria, which bind nitrogen from the air, contributing to soil fertilisation. Unlike the Garden Pea, all parts of the Meadow Pea are slightly poisonous.

Birdsfoot Trefoil
Lotus corniculatus

DISTINGUISHING FEATURES: Birdsfoot Trefoil can grow up to 50cm tall and has pinnate leaves with five leaflets, of which the first leaflet pair is attached directly to the plant stem ③. The sun-yellow flowers form in long-stemmed umbellate clusters at the end of the stems ①. The fruits, which hang off the stem like claws ②, appear after flowering.

DISTRIBUTION: Birdsfoot Trefoil is common on meadows and heathland.

TYPICAL FEATURES
The butterfly-like flowers of Birdsfoot Trefoil are reddish on the outside, particularly when in the bud.

OTHER: The stem is anchored in the ground by long taproots. The rootstock can live for up to 30 years. Birdsfoot Trefoil is valued as fodder for grazing livestock and for bees. The pollination mechanism of the flowers is specially designed for bees and bumblebees.

SIMILAR SPECIES: Horseshoe Vetch (*Hippocrepis comosa*) ④ grows on limestone soil in unfertilised meadows and on cliffs. Its fruits consist of 3–6 horseshoe-shaped parts. It is widespread and common throughout Europe.

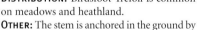

163

Field Pansy
Viola arvensis

DISTINGUISHING FEATURES: Field Pansy is normally only 10–20cm high and has long-stemmed white, yellow or violet-tinged flowers on a heavily branching stem. The lower petal has a spur and is patterned with dark stripes that point towards the centre of the flower ①. The broad leaves near the top of the stem are elongated and lobed ③, with stalks growing near the base of the plant ②.

DISTRIBUTION: Common on fields and rubbish tips, beside footpaths and on wasteland.

TYPICAL FEATURES
The creamy-yellow petals of the Field Pansy face upwards and are the same length or only slightly longer than the sepals.

OTHER: Field Pansy is a very hardy species. The roots can be 45cm deep. In traditional medicine it is used to cure coughs and throat inflammation.

SIMILAR SPECIES: Wild Pansy (*Viola tricolor*) ④ has larger flowers, normally with a more blue-violet colour, although it may even have three colours. The petals are much longer than the sepals.

Downy Hemp-nettle
Galeopsis segetum

DISTINGUISHING FEATURES: Downy Hemp-nettle is an annual that can reach a height of 10–40cm. It has a branching, quadrangular stem. Opposite leaves can be up to 4cm long. They have a short stalk and coarsely serrated edges, reminiscent of the Nettle ③. The underside of the leaves is densely hairy, but their upper surfaces only have a few short hairs. The yellow flowers form in dense whorls in the axils of the upper leaves ①. The flower is about 3cm long, with a hood-like upper lip

TYPICAL FEATURES
On the lower lip, at the entrance to the petal tube, there are two small 'teeth' which are characteristic of Hemp-nettle species.

and a three-part lower lip. The median lips are large with dark spots ②.

DISTRIBUTION: On woodland edges, in light woodland and on wasteland; on sandy soils.

SIMILAR SPECIES: Large-flowered Hemp-nettle (*Galeopsis speciosa*) ④ can grow up to 1m in height. The broad, median lips of the flowers are dark-red to bright violet. The species is found extensively growing in hedgerows, beside fields and footpaths, and on wasteland.

Common Toadflax
Linaria vulgaris

DISTINGUISHING FEATURES: Common Toad-flax is 20–70cm tall ① and is conspicuous due to its long, soft, narrow, needle-like leaves ③ and the flower cluster at the tip of the stem ④. This cluster consists of individual yellow flowers with a two-part upper lip and a three-part lower lip ②. The middle section of the lower lip is padded like a cushion and has a bright orange colour.

DISTRIBUTION: On railway embankments, rubbish tips, footpaths and similar habitats.

TYPICAL FEATURES
The neck of the light-yellow flower is elongated to form a noticeable spur, in which the nectar collects.

OTHER: Only larger insects, such as bumble-bees, are able to enter the neck of the flower between the upper and lower lips. Common Toadflax has branching roots which extend up to 1m deep into the soil. These roots can store water for a long time, even in droughts. When this herbaceous perennial is dug up, a part of the root often remains in the soil, and this can develop into a new plant.

Common Cow Wheat
Melampyrum pratense

DISTINGUISHING FEATURES: The vertical, angular stem of the 10–30cm tall Common Cow Wheat is occasionally branched. Its opposite leaves are elongated and narrow ③. The pale yellow flowers form clusters like an ear of corn ①, and have a long flower tube, a hood-like upper lip and a lower lip which protrudes horizontally ②.

DISTRIBUTION: The plant prefers light woodland, heathland and high moors. It indicates that the soil is nutrient-poor and acidic.

TYPICAL FEATURES
The flowers of Common Cow Wheat stand away from the stem, almost at a right angle. All flowers point in the same direction ①.

OTHER: Common Cow Wheat is poisonous and semi-parasitic. It can produce its own chlorophyll but absorbs nutrients from the roots of other plants and grasses using nodular sucking organs.

SIMILAR SPECIES: *Melampyrum nemorosum* ④ also has yellow flowers but can be distinguished by its broader leaves and violet stipules with deep serrations, which form in the flower cluster.

Hairy Yellow Rattle
Rhinanthus alectorolophus

DISTINGUISHING FEATURES: This plant can reach a height of 20–50cm and has yellow, lipped flowers ②, which always form in the axils of the pale-green leaves at the top of the stem ①. The upper lip has a small, blue, tooth-like protrusion. The convex calyx is also conspicuous. The oval, serrated leaves have an opposite arrangement on the stem ③.

TYPICAL FEATURES
The hairy stem, upper leaves and calyx of the Hairy Yellow Rattle are what gives it its name. The calyx extends slightly over the wrinkled petal tube.

DISTRIBUTION: Hairy Yellow Rattle often covers large areas in meadows.

OTHER: The plant's name derives from the sound caused by the seeds rattling inside the fruit. It is semi-parasitic, like the Common Cow Wheat (p166). If it grows in large numbers, it can inhibit the growth of other meadow plants and grasses. The plant is slightly poisonous for grazing animals.

SIMILAR SPECIES: *Rhinanthus glacialis* ④ grows in mountains on stony grassland. Its upper leaves have long hairs.

Lesser Yellow Rattle
Rhinanthus minor

DISTINGUISHING FEATURES: This plant can be 10–30cm tall and has narrow, serrated leaves ①. The rounded calyx has no hairs and holds a light-yellow, lipped flower ②. The flower tube is straight, and the two teeth on the upper leaf are white or pale-blue.

TYPICAL FEATURES
Lesser Yellow Rattle differs from Greater Yellow Rattle in its straight petal tube, the entrance to which is wide open.

DISTRIBUTION: On nutrient-poor meadows, heathland and unfertilised grassland in lowland areas.

OTHER: Lesser Yellow Rattle is also poisonous and semi-parasitic. The capsule fruits remain surrounded by the inflated calyx. Even months after flowering, the hard, greyish-brown fruits can be found with the seeds rattling inside. The Yellow Rattle often flowers again in late summer.

SIMILAR SPECIES: Greater Yellow Rattle *(Rhinanthus angustifolius)* ④ has a hairless calyx. The entrance to the upward-pointing, wrinkled neck of the flower is almost completely closed ③.

169

Jupiter's Distaff
Salvia glutinosa

DISTINGUISHING FEATURES: Jupiter's Distaff has large leaves with an arrow-shaped base and serrated edges ②. The angular stem is slightly woody at the base and can grow up to 1m high. Whorls of lipped flowers form at the tip of the stem in upright, raceme-like clusters ①.

DISTRIBUTION: In woodland, in mountains and gorges.

OTHER: Jupiter's Distaff is almost shrub-like, due to the many branches and woody stem base. In winter, however, most of the plant above the ground dies back, and the plant grows new shoots from the base in spring. Jupiter's Distaff, unlike related species, does not smell of sage, and has no medicinal uses.

SIMILAR SPECIES: Yellow Woundwort (*Stachys recta*) ④ grows in meadows, in woodland edges and coppices. Its leaves are hairy ③, and the white-yellow flowers are much smaller than Jupiter's Distaff.

> **TYPICAL FEATURES**
> Jupiter's Distaff has red-brown patterning on the lower lip of the flower. The whole flower feels sticky.

Yellow Deadnettle
Yellow Archangel
Lamiastrum galeobdolon ssp. *montanum*

DISTINGUISHING FEATURES: Yellow Deadnettle is 30–50cm tall and has a quadrangular, upright stem, with perpendicular hairs at the base ①. The nettle-like serrated leaves ② are arranged opposite each other in pairs. Whorls of golden yellow flowers form in the leaf axils ④, and the lower lip of the flower has orange striping ③. The plant reproduces using long, creeping shoots.

DISTRIBUTION: Yellow Deadnettle often forms in large clumps in deciduous woodland that is not too dry.

OTHER: This plant often retains its leaves in winter and does not bloom until its second or third year. The shoots curve downwards and the leaf nodes in contact with the ground quickly form roots, enabling the plant to cover large areas very quickly, especially if there is a lot of shade. A cultivated variety of the plant with silver, white flecked leaves is grown in cottage gardens. This variety is now found in the wild.

> **TYPICAL FEATURES**
> Yellow Deadnettle is the only plant with nettle-like leaves that also has yellow flowers.

Yellow Balsam
Touch-me-not | *Impatiens noli-tangere*

DISTINGUISHING FEATURES: Yellow Balsam has a smooth, almost transparent stem, which can reach a height of 70cm ①. The oval leaves are slightly serrated ② and become slightly crinkly in high temperatures or in drought. The lemon-yellow flowers have an unusual shape and hang from thin stalks ④. The flowers have a thin, wrinkled spur.

DISTRIBUTION: The plant prefers shady habitats and is commonly found in woodland and beside shaded footpaths with a humid atmosphere and damp soil.

OTHER: When ripe, the capsule fruit ③ bursts open at the slightest touch, catapulting the seeds great distances. The Latin name *noli-tangere*, sometimes *noli me tangere*, means 'Touch-me-not' – hence the flower's common name.

TYPICAL FEATURES
Yellow Balsam is easy to distinguish by its large, yellow flowers, oval serrated leaves and typical fruits.

Yellow Iris
Yellow Flag | *Iris pseudacorus*

DISTINGUISHING FEATURES: This eye-catching marsh plant has long, sword-shaped leaves and can reach a height of 50–100cm ①. The yellow flowers form individually on a round stalk and have six petals and three, large petal-like stigma ④. The plant forms long, elongated capsule fruits ②.

DISTRIBUTION: The Yellow Iris is protected and grows in various damp habitats, such as on the banks of stagnant or slow-flowing waterways and in alluvial forests, particularly of alder. It is the commonest European species of iris and can cover large areas.

TYPICAL FEATURES
The Yellow Iris is the only species of iris native to Europe. It has bright-yellow flowers. The flower colour, size and habitat make it unmistakeable.

OTHER: The plant is very undemanding and is often grown in garden ponds. It contains essential oils, fibrin and tannins and some toxins, which have a peppery taste and persist, even when the plant is dried. The thick, creeping roots ③ were once used in combination with iron ore to make a black dye.

173

Lady's Mantle
Alchemilla vulgaris

DISTINGUISHING FEATURES: Lady's Mantle can vary in size between 25 and 50cm. It has characteristic round- to kidney-shaped leaves, that are folded like pockets ③. The greenish-yellow flowers are small and inconspicuous ②. They form in a dense, knot-like cluster on the end of the horizontal or vertical stem ①.

TYPICAL FEATURES
Lady's Mantle flowers do not have colourful petals. They consist of four green sepals and four outer sepals ②.

DISTRIBUTION: Lady's Mantle is common in fertilised fields, heathland, coppices and grassy areas beside footpaths, but it needs a damp environment. Rare in lowland areas, but quite common on high ground.

OTHER: Water droplets often fall on Lady's Mantle leaves, and hang from the leaf edges like pearls ④. If the air is very humid, the plant releases water from pores in its leaves.

Spiked Rampion
Phyteuma spicatum

DISTINGUISHING FEATURES: The long, greenish-white flower clusters form on a stem which can be up to 70cm tall ①. Before blooming, the five-petalled flowers curl up like claws or spikes. The long-stalked basal leaves are heart-shaped ②, but the elongated leaves on the stem have only short stalks or are attached directly to the stem ③.

TYPICAL FEATURES
Spiked Rampion has a small number of leaves with an alternating arrangement. Lower leaves often have black flecks.

DISTRIBUTION: Spiked Rampion prefers deciduous and mixed woodland with dense vegetation and mountain meadows. It can be found in the Alps up to an altitude of 2,100m.

OTHER: Spiked Rampion is noticeable because its flower clusters seem to continue flowering forever. The long clusters form ever more individual flowers at the tip, while fruit capsules develop near the base ④. The plant produces a milky sap. An infusion made from the turnip-like roots is used in traditional medicine to treat gallstones.

175

Narrow-leaved Plantain

Plantago lanceolata

DISTINGUISHING FEATURES: Narrow-leaved Plantain commonly grows in meadows. The long, narrow leaves mainly grow upwards from a basal rosette. They are lanceolate in shape and covered in silky hairs, tapering towards the stalk which has a grooved cross-section ②. The short, brownish-white flower heads form well above the leaves on forked stalks 50cm high ①.

DISTRIBUTION: Very common on both fertilised and unfertilised meadows and in pastures with nutrient-rich soil; also beside footpaths.

TYPICAL FEATURES

The inconspicuous flowers form in heads like ears of corn ④. The stamens protrude way beyond the flower head. They are white at first, but later turn brown ③.

OTHER: Narrow-leaved Plantain is an ancient medicinal plant. It is said to loosen mucous and help treat coughs. The flowers have no nectar, but they are sometime pollinated by insects, which collect the pollen.

Greater Plantain

Plantago major

DISTINGUISHING FEATURES: Greater Plantain can reach a height of 40cm and has broad, tough, hairless leaves, with a long stalk ②. The inconspicuous flowers form in long, dense, green flower heads ①. Reddish lilac-coloured anthers, later turning yellow, extend beyond the whitish sepals.

DISTRIBUTION: The plant is very hardy and is widely distributed worldwide, often covering large areas in places where there is dense undergrowth. It is often found on playing fields and lawns and beside footpaths.

TYPICAL FEATURES

The broad, rounded leaves of the Greater Plantain have three to seven prominent veins. These can be taken out when you tear up the leaves.

OTHER: The plant was introduced into North America by the Europeans. Native Americans call the plant 'Footsteps of the White Man'. It can establish itself very quickly.

SIMILAR SPECIES: Hoary Plantain (*Plantago media*) ④ grows in dry meadows and heathland. It has fragrant, lilac flowers and slightly narrower leaves with no stems or short stems ③.

Sun Spurge
Euphorbia helioscopia

DISTINGUISHING FEATURES: Sun Spurge has a 15–30cm-long stem with oval leaves, which are only serrated towards their tip ②. The light-green, umbellate flower cluster has five branches, surrounded by stipules of the same colour ①. The flowers face the sun. Although the flower cluster consists of many reduced flowers without petals ③, the light-green stipules give the impression that the head is large.

TYPICAL FEATURES
By the time it flowers, the leaves on the stem of the Sun Spurge are already yellowing, and have fallen at the plant base.

DISTRIBUTION: In sunny locations beside fields and footpaths.

OTHER: Sun Spurge has a poisonous milky-white sap. The smooth fruit capsules each contain three seeds. When ripe they burst open with a pop and catapult the seeds away.

SIMILAR SPECIES: Sweet Spurge *(Euphorbia dulcis)* ④ is larger and grows in woodland. The dark-green leaves are blue-green on the underside, and are elongated, tapering towards the stalk.

Purple Spurge
Euphorbia peplus

DISTINGUISHING FEATURES: Purple Spurge is small and delicate and reaches a maximum height of 30cm ①. The stem is covered with pale green, smooth-edged leaves ②. The small flower umbel usually has three branches. As with all types of Spurge, this species has pseudo-flowers with a five-pointed calyx containing several stamens and an ovary. There are half-moon shaped pores around the outside that release nectar. Three-part capsule fruits form after flowering, each part having two ridges ④.

TYPICAL FEATURES
The sepals on the Purple Spurge form in pairs and are broadly triangular in shape ③.

DISTRIBUTION: This short-lived plant grows in fields and gardens.

OTHER: The plant dies as soon as it has formed its seeds. Only the seeds survive. In mild winters, the plant can germinate very early, meaning that several generations can grow in one year. In gardens where the soil is frequently disturbed, Purple Spurge can often cover large areas. All parts of the plant contain a poisonous, white, milky sap.

Cypress Spurge
Euphorbia cyparissias

DISTINGUISHING FEATURES: Cypress Spurge can grow to a height of 30cm and has green-yellow flower clusters, forming an umbel ①. The leaves can be up to 3cm long and are needle-shaped and thin, but soft ②.

DISTRIBUTION: On embankments and at the foot of cliffs, on dry, limestone, unfertilised meadows, and in light, dry woodland.

OTHER: The plant can be attacked by a microscopic fungus known as *Uromyces pisi-sativi* fungus, of which it is an intermediate host. It then has a completely different appearance. The stem is weak and unbranched, the leaves become broader, and orange pustules, containing the fungus spores, form on the underside of the leaves.

SIMILAR SPECIES: *Euphorbia verrucosa* usually grows in clumps and has broader leaves ③ than the Cypress Spurge. Its fruits ④ can be identified by their warty surface.

TYPICAL FEATURES
The flower clusters of Cypress Spurge form in an umbel with four branches. The fruits are bright red.

Pineapple Weed
Chamomilla suaveolens

DISTINGUISHING FEATURES: Pineapple Weed can reach a height of 15–40cm and is a species of chamomile. It has oval, green-yellow flower heads ①. The sepals form in several rows around the flower clusters and are edged with a paler colour ④. The branching stem has delicate, pinnate leaves, each leaflet being divided into two or three parts ②.

DISTRIBUTION: The plant grows beside footpaths, in rubbish tips and on lawns, mainly near towns and cities. Pineapple Weed is native to Siberia and North America. It has spread quickly throughout Europe since the mid 19th century, particularly along railway routes.

OTHER: This species of chamomile can survive being trampled under foot. It uses clinging fruits to disperse its seeds. Pineapple Weed has the characteristic aroma of chamomile but it cannot be used as a substitute for chamomile for infusions and in traditional medicine.

TYPICAL FEATURES
Pineapple Weed can be easily distinguished from other species of chamomile because it does not have any white ray flowers. Its domed flower heads are hollow ③.

Mugwort

Artemisia vulgaris

DISTINGUISHING FEATURES: This plant grows upright and can reach a height of 50–150cm ①. The angular, branching stem has sparse hairs and often has a reddish colour. The pinnate leaves ③ are dark green and hairless on the upper surface, but have white, matted hairs on the underside. The numerous small flower heads form in ears at the tip of the stem ②. They are green or yellow-brown and contain only disc flowers.

TYPICAL FEATURES
Mugwort leaves contain bitter alkaloids and essential oils, which release an aromatic fragrance when rubbed.

DISTRIBUTION: Forms large clumps in rubbish tips, weed beds and bank undergrowth.

OTHER: Mugwort is an old medicinal plant. Fresh or dried leaves can also be used as a kitchen herb.

SIMILAR SPECIES: Wormwood (*Artemisia absinthium*) ④ can be identified by its white, felt-like hairs which give its leaves a silver-grey appearance on both sides. Strong aromatic fragrance when rubbed.

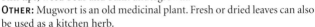

Cabbage Thistle

Cirsium oleraceum

DISTINGUISHING FEATURES: Cabbage Thistle can reach a height of 1.5m and has yellow-white composite flowers consisting solely of disc flowers ③. They are surrounded by pale-green leaves which look like cabbage leaves ①. The soft, elongated leaves near the plant base are pinnate and surround the stem ②.

TYPICAL FEATURES
The light-green leaves of the Cabbage Thistle have soft spines like long hairs. They are not very spiky.

DISTRIBUTION: The plant prefers damp meadows, flat moorland and ditches. It can first be seen in May or June, after the first hay-making.

OTHER: The flowers are not only a source of food for many insects, they also provide shelter for animals. Earwigs often hide in the upper leaves near the flowers.

SIMILAR SPECIES: Yellow Melancholy Thistle (*Cirsium erisithales*), grows in mountain woodland and on woodland edges and has light-yellow flower heads ④. Its stem has sticky hairs near the top.

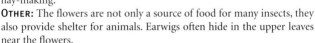

183

Gallant Soldier
Galinsoga ciliata

DISTINGUISHING FEATURES: Gallant Soldier can grow up to 50cm tall and has tiny flowers ① consisting of yellow disc flowers and white ray flowers ③. The branching stem has hairs, which stand out at right-angles, particularly near the flowers. The pointed oval leaves ② have an opposite arrangement.

DISTRIBUTION: On fallow land, in fields and gardens and in rubbish tips.

OTHER: Gallant Soldier was introduced to Europe in the 19th century from Central and South America and continues to spread throughout Europe. In good years, it can produce two or more generations. As a result of its origins, the plant is very sensitive to frost but the seeds can survive harsh winters, enabling new plants to germinate in the spring.

SIMILAR SPECIES: Small-flowered Galinsoga *(Galinsoga parviflora)* ④ has a stem which is bald, or only slightly hairy.

TYPICAL FEATURES
The tiny white ray flowers form in groups of five around the similarly small, green-yellow disc flowers ③.

Common Nettle
Urtica dioica

DISTINGUISHING FEATURES: This herbaceous perennial can reach 30–150cm. It has a vertical, quadrangular stem, which only rarely branches ①. The oval, sharply serrated leaves form on stalks in an opposite arrangement. Stem and leaves are densely covered in hairs, including stinging hairs ③. Male and female flowers form on different plants. Male flowers form in vertical panicles in the leaf axils; female flowers ② hang downwards after pollination.

DISTRIBUTION: By footpaths, on wasteland and rubbish dumps near towns; indicative of nitrogen-rich soil; very common.

OTHER: The green parts of Common Nettle contain flavonoids, vitamins and plant acids. Young Common Nettle leaves can be prepared in a similar way to spinach and are also drunk as an infusion. The sting can be a dangerous irritant to those who are sensitive to it.

SIMILAR SPECIES: Small Nettle *(Urtica urens)* ④ is an annual plant that only reaches a height of 5cm. It has rounder, smaller leaves.

TYPICAL FEATURES
The Common Nettle can be easily identified by its height and by its serrated leaves, but especially by its stinging hairs.

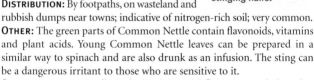

185

Index

Acknowledgements

Front cover photos: Primrose; small pictures from left: Large-flowered Eyebright, Carthusian Pink, Wood Forget-me-not
Pages 6/7: Summer Meadow
Pages 24/25: Cuckoo Flower

Bleinagel: 19 bot. mi. l.; blickwinkel: (Perseke) 16, 22 l. top, r. top, 151 top l., 153 bot. r., 155 bot.l., 159 bot. r., 161 top l., 171 top l., (Schaber) 23 r. mi. top, (Tomm) 9 l. top, l. mi.; Diedrich: 15 mi., 21 mi. bot., 51 bot. r.; Eisenbeiss: 9 r., 13 r. bot., 18 mi. r., 29 top r., 35 top r., bot. r., 37 bot. l., 41 top l., 43 top l., 47 top r., bot. r., 49 bot.l., bot. r., 59 bot. r., 61 top l., 81 bot.l., 99 top l., 103 top r., bot. r., 105 bot. l., 109 top, 119 top l., top r., 123 top l., bot. l., 135 bot. l., 143 top r., 145 top l., 157 bot. l., 171 bot. l., bot. r., 173 bot. r., 181 top l., 183 top r., 185 bot.; Garnweidner: 11 top, 18 l., mi. l., 37 bot. l., 45 top l., 109 bot. r., 113 bot. r., 131 top l., top r., 137 top r., bot. r., 141 top r., 165 bot. r., 169 bot. l.; Giel: 75 top r., 81 bot. r., U 4 r; Himmelhuber: 69 top; Hinz: 53 top r., 57 top l., 71 top l., top r., 87 top r., 91 top r., 93 top r., 115 top r., 117 bot. l., 121 bot. r., 127 top l., 147 top r., 161 bot.; Hofrichter: U 2 bot., 8, 10 bot. mi., 19 bot. r., 23 r. mi. bot., 95 top r., 133 top r., 143 bot. r., 145 top l.; Krmer: Page 65 bot. r.; Labhardt: 2 mi., 3 top; Lauber: 23 r. bot., 29 bot. l., bot. r., 31 bot.l., 33 bot., 41 top r., 45 top r., 67 bot. r., 73 top r., 77 bot. r., 79 bot. r., 83 bot. r., 91 bot. r., 105 bot. r., 109 top l., 111 bot. r., 113 top r., bot. l., 117 top r., 147 bot. r., 149 bot. r., 155 bot. r., 157 bot. r., 161 top r., 163 top r., 169 top l., 177 top l., 179 bot. r., 181 top r., bot. r., 185 top r.; Laux: 55 top l., bot. r., 61 bot. r., 71 bot. r., 125 top r., 139 top l., bot. r., 153 top l., top r., 167 top r., 185 bot. r.; Limbrunner: 53 top l., 79 bot. l., 83 top r., 89 top r.; Marktanner: 33 top, top l., bot. r., 133 bot. r.; Pforr: U 1 (large picture), top l., top r., U 2 l. top, 9 l.bot., 10 bot. l., bot. r., 13 r. top, 14, 15 bot., 19 bot. l., 21 mi. top, bot., 23 l. mi. top, 27 top l., top r., 31 top l., 37 top l., top r., 39 top, 45 bot., bot. r., 47 bot. l., 49 top r., 51 bot. l., 53 bot. l., 57 top l., 59 top r., 63 bot. r., 65 bot. l., 69 top l., 73 top l., bot. l., bot. r., 75 top l., bot. r., 77 top l., top r., bot. r., 79 top r., 83 top l., bot., 85 top r., bot. r., 87 bot. l., 91 bot. l., 95 top l., bot. r., 97 top r., bot. r., 99 bot. l., 101 bot. r., 105 top r., top l., 107 top l., 109 bot., 111 top l., bot. l., 113 top l., 115 bot. r., 117 top l., 121 bot. l., 125 top r., 127 top, bot., 129 top r., bot. r., 131 bot. l., 133 top l., 135 top r., 137 bot., 139 top, bot., 141 bot. r., 143 top l., bot. l., 145 bot. r.,147 top l, 151 top r., bot. l., 153 bot. l., 155 top l., bot. r., 157 top l., 159 top l., bot. l., 161 bot. r., 163 bot. l., 165 top l., top r., 173 top r., 175 top l., bot. r., 177 bot. r., 183 top l., U 4 mi.; Popp: 20 top; Reinhard, H.: U 2 r. top, 2 bot., 6/7, 10 top, 19 top, bot. mi. r., 20 mi. top, mi. bot., 21 top, 22 l.bot., 23 l. top, l. mi. bot., r. top, 29 top l., 35 top l., bot. l., 39 bot. l., bot. r., mi. bot., 41 bot. l., 43 bot. l., 47 top l., 49 top l., 51 top r., 55 bot. l., 57 bot. r., 67 top r., 71 bot. l., 81 top l., top r., 85 top l., bot.l., 91 top l., 93 bot. l., bot. r., 95 top l., 97 top l., 99 top r., 101 top r., 103 top l., bot. l., 107 top l., 115 top l., bot. l., 119 bot. l., 129 top l., bot. l., 135 top l., 141 top l., 147 bot. l., 157 top, 159 top, 175 bot. l., 177 bot. l., 183 bot. l., bot. r.; Reinhard, N.: 89 bot. r., 119 bot. r., 133 bot. l., 149 top l., 163 bot. r., 173 bot. l.; Schrmpp: U 2 r. mi., 20 bot., 27 bot. r., 31 bot. r., 41 bot. r., 43 top r., 53 bot. r., 55 top r., 61 bot. r., 63 bot. r., 75 bot. l., 79 top l., 99 bot. r., 101 top l., 109 bot. r., 111 top r., 123 top, 125 bot. l., 145 bot. l., 149 bot. l., 165 bot. l., 167 bot. r., 179 top l., top r., 185 top l.; Silvestris online: (Bohler) 51 top l., (Giel) 22 r. bot., (Gross) 3 bot.,181 bot. l., (Hecker) 67 top r., 121 top r., (Heppner) 69 bot. r., 149 top r., (Jacobi) 11 mi. bot., 13 l.bot., 15 top, (Kuch) 67 bot. r., 89 top l., (Partsch) 59 top l., (Roland) 131 bot. r., (Schweinsberg) 97 bot. l., (Singer) 167 bot. l., (Skibbe) 11 bot., (Sohns) 69 bot., (Usher) 11 mi. top, (Wagner) 141 bot. r., 169 bot. r., (Willner) 107 bot. r., (Wothe) 171 top r.; Stein: U 1 top mi., 2 top; Willner, O.: U 2 l. mi., 59 bot. l., 65 top r., 93 top l.; Willner, W.: 13 l. top, 24/25, 43 bot. r., 57 bot. l., 63 bot. l., 65 top l., 87 top l., 89 bot. l., 107 top r., 117 bot. r., 123 bot. r., 125 bot. r., 167 top l., 175 top r., 177 top r., 179 bot. l.; Zeininger: 63 top l., 121 top l., 127 bot., 169 top l., 173 top l.; Zepf, E.: 23 l. bot., 27 bot. l., 163 top l.

191

Disclaimer

The dates and facts in this guide have been researched checked with great care. No gurantee can, however, be given, and the pub cepts no liability for damage to people, property or assets.

This edition first published in 2006 by New Holland Publishers (UK) Ltd
London • Cape Town • Sydney • Auckland
10 9 8 7 6 5 4 3 2 1
www.newhollandpublishers.com
Garfield House, 86–88 Edgware Road, London, W2 2EA, UK

ISBN 1 84537 473 8

Publishing Manager: Jo Hemmings
Senior Editor: Kate Michell
Assistant Editor: Kate Parker
Translator: American Pie, London and California

Series editor: Steffen Haselbach
Editor-in-chief: Anita Zellner
Desk editors: Dr. Michael Eppinger, Dr. Helga Hofmann
Cover design: independent Medien-Design
Layout: H. Bornemann Design
Illustrations: Peter Braun, atelier amAldi
Film: Filmsatz Schröter, Munich
Production: Petra Roth
Repro: Penta, Munich
Printing: Appl, Wemding
Binding: Auer, Donauwörth

Printed in Germany